Internet Primer

Internet Primer

For Information Professionals

A Basic Guide to Internet Networking Technology

BY ELIZABETH LANE AND CRAIG SUMMERHILL

Meckler

Westport • London • Melbourne

Library of Congress Cataloging-in-Publication Data

Lane, Elizabeth S.
    Internet Primer for information professionals : a basic guide
to Internet networking technology / Elizabeth Lane and Craig
Summerhill.
      p. cm.
    Includes bibliographical references and index.
    ISBN 0-88736-831-X $
    1. Internet (Computer network)   I. Summerhill, Craig. II. Title.
TK5105.875.I57L35 1993
004.6'7–dc20   92-36183
                                   CIP

British Library Cataloguing-in-Publication Data

Lane, Elizabeth S.
  Internet Primer for Information
  Professionals: Basic Guide to Internet
  Networking Technology.
  I. Title. II. Summerhill, Craig
  004.6

  ISBN 0-88736-831-X

Meckler Publishing, the publishing division of Meckler Corporation,
  11 Ferry Lane West, Westport, CT 06880.
Meckler Ltd., Artillery House, Artillery Row, London SW1P 1RT, U.K.
Meckler, GPO Box 61A, Melbourne, Victoria, Australia 3001

Printed on acid free paper.
Printed and bound in the United States of America.

Contents

Introduction

The many national and international networks that make up what we currently call "The Internet" are of increasing importance in business, education, and library science. The role of electronic communication in commerce, research, and in all levels of education from K-12 through graduate study, is growing by leaps and bounds.

Although networks bring great gifts to those that use them, they also carry a great risk: that barriers to network access, primarily in the areas of cost and ease-of-use, will result in an increasing gap between "information haves" and "information have-nots."

This book is intended for those who could benefit from the many uses of the emerging global network, but who have not yet been presented with the opportunity to learn of its resources or applicability to their work. It provides a starting point—a "broad brush" overview of the networks, their uses, and their potential—which will enable even the newest computer and network users to take their first steps toward utilization of these tools.

Several excellent introductory publications on the Internet currently exist (for more information on some of these publications, see Chapter Five, which describes resources, and the Bibliography). However, many of these publications share a serious drawback for those who are not yet connected to the network. Their limited distribution channels—primarily over the Internet itself—make it unlikely that they will be seen by the "network neophytes" who need them most.

Publication over the networks is a powerful distribution method; it allows for quick, inexpensive dissemination of materials, and for easy updating of documents. However, for those who have not yet learned how to access or effectively use network applications and resources, these network-based publications might just as well not exist.

This book is designed to reach newcomers to the networks. It provides a first look at what the networks are, how they work, and what they offer to users. The network world changes so quickly that many things in this book will be slightly outdated before it even goes into print. However, it is important nonetheless to make this information available in a format that does not require access to advanced technological tools and training.

We begin in Chapter One by describing and defining what the Internet is, and looking at the legislation for and beginning development of the proposed and the interim National Research and Education Network (NREN). Chapter Two follows up on this discussion by briefly describing some of the many networks that make up or connect to the Internet, and suggesting channels for institutions and individuals to pursue in order to obtain access to the networks.

Chapter Three provides a brief introduction to the technology that underlies the networks. Although it is not necessary to be a telecommunications expert to use the networks, it is helpful for librarians and educators to understand enough of the technology to allow them to be involved in the planning and implementation of the NREN.

Chapter Four looks at some of the application programs that can be used to access the network, and to utilize the many resources it provides. Examples from a variety of operating environments are provided, including both host systems (IBM and UNIX™ hosts), and desktop systems (Macintosh, IBM-PC, and workstations). In addition to describing commonly used applications—electronic mail, FTP, and Telnet—we look at some of the emerging client-server models for applications, such as WAIS servers and the Internet Gopher.

Applications are only tools to access information, and Chapter Five describes some of the many information resources that can be accessed over the networks. We look at publications designed to help users navigate the networks, as well as some of the library catalogs, software archives, and organizations currently available.

Finally, in Chapter Six, we examine some of the policy issues that are affecting the use and design of telecommunications networks. These issues include access, and barriers to access; conflicts between different network constituencies; the costs associated with building and using network resources; and security considerations that arise as resources are made available to a broader community.

Chapter One: What Is the Internet?

The Internet and Inter-networking

Over the past decade, the terms "Internet" and "inter-networked" have begun to appear with increasing regularity in the vocabulary of computer users worldwide. These terms are becoming almost commonplace, particularly in higher educational computing and in the library profession. Internet, inter-networking, and related technical terms—which would have been considered obscure jargon by most academics as recently as five years ago—are now appearing in popular periodicals like *MacWorld*, *PC Magazine*, and *Scientific American*. Within the higher education community, references to the Internet are no longer restricted to computer science and electronic engineering literature, but now appear with regularity in disciplines that include the social sciences and the humanities.

What is the Internet? And what is inter-networking? Generally, when one encounters Internet spelled with a capital "I," the reference is to an existing worldwide communications system linking together thousands of computers. The computers that make up the Internet are owned and operated by the U. S. government, colleges and universities, public libraries, public schools, small businesses, private corporations, and not-for-profit organizations. The people using these computers are computer scientists, librarians, university administrators, businesspeople, doctors, lawyers, students, and researchers from virtually every discipline.

At first glance, the Internet may appear as a single mammoth network. In reality, though, the network is an intricate series of smaller networks inter-operating to exchange data between the computers (hosts) on the network(s). In fact, this inter-operability, the ability of many different types of computers to exchange data, is a great strength of the Internet and the technology on which it is based. Although the many networks comprising the Internet are distinct entities politically, economically, or technically, the vast majority of the computers on the Internet share a common set of computer telecommunications protocols that allow them to inter-operate.

The core suite of protocols making this interaction possible is the Transmission Control Protocol/Internet Protocol (TCP/IP). When a number of computers are using these protocols to communicate, they are said to be "inter-networking." It is possible for a small network of computers to be using the TCP/IP protocols without being connected to the Internet; however, the main incentive for developing a local area network based on the TCP/IP protocol suite is to provide seamless inter-operability with the larger conglomerate of hosts comprising the Internet.

Among the activities commonly occurring in the Internet are:

- exchange of electronic mail and data files in a wide-area environment;
- on-line "real-time" interaction with other network users;
- participation in electronic mailing lists and conferences;
- receipt of electronic publications;

- access to data stored on remote computers;
- access to remote scientific computing peripherals such as supercomputers, remote sensing equipment, telescopes, and graphics processors; and
- access to a wide selection of pubic domain and shareware software.

Advanced Research Projects Agency (ARPA)/(DARPA)

The first inter-network was built by the U.S. Department of Defense, and was called the Advanced Research Projects Agency (ARPA) network, or ARPAnet (later referred to as the DARPAnet). The development of the ARPAnet began in the late 1960s as a relatively small research experiment designed to demonstrate the viability of packet-switch technology (detailed information on packet-switching is provided in Chapter Three). The original ARPAnet used 8-bit (1 byte) addressing, and therefore could connect a maximum of only sixty-four computers, a number which seems amusingly small in retrospect.

In the mid-1970s, the TCP/IP protocols were developed for use on the ARPAnet. Prior to this, the network had used a telecommunications protocol referred to as the Network Control Protocol. With the development of IP addressing, the number of network addresses was expanded to the current 32 bits (4 bytes), and a series of network classes were instituted to provide for the addressing of an even greater number of computers (see Chapter Three for more information on IP addressing). Using this 32-bit addressing scheme, hundreds of thousands of computers can be uniquely identified in the network's address space.

One might assume that the primary use of the ARPAnet was for the development of "top-secret" military projects, and, in fact, the network was originally envisioned to play such a role in U.S. military activities. However, relatively early in the project, ARPA discovered that the network offered a cost-effective mechanism for scientists and researchers to communicate electronically. Although ARPAnet has been officially disbanded (ARPA was dismantled in 1988/1989), this role as a communications channel for scholars and researchers remains prominent in the TCP/IP Internet. ARPA must be credited with providing funding to allow the creation of a generally applicable knowledge base on high-speed computer networking. Much of the current research and development in computer networking is still directly attributable to ARPA's early work.

The National Science Foundation Network (NSFnet)

If ARPA deserves credit for the existence of an emerging global data network, the U.S. National Science Foundation (NSF) must be equally recognized. In the early 1980s, the NSF began to develop a series of programs centered on the opportunities that powerful supercomputing equipment offered to scientific research in areas such as global weather modeling, medical imaging, and molecular physics.

In 1984, the NSF undertook a project to fund and link several supercomputer research centers throughout the United States, using communications lines leased from commercial telephone service providers. Additionally, in 1985, an agreement was reached between the NSF and ARPA allowing for closer corroboration between ARPA researchers and NSF-funded supercomputing sites. Among the earliest supercomputer research centers to be linked were such widely dispersed sites as the San Diego Supercomputer Center at the University of California-San Diego, the National Center for Supercomputer Applications at the University of Illinois at Champaign-Urbana, and the John von Neumann Supercomputer Center at Princeton University.

In November 1987, Merit Networking, Inc. of Ann Arbor, Michigan, entered into a cooperative agreement with the NSF to re-engineer and expand the supercomputer network begun earlier in the decade. With the completion of this agreement, Merit assumed managerial responsibility for the operation of the National Science Foundation Network (NSFnet) for a period of five years. Merit then entered into a partnership with two large technology-based corporations, MCI and IBM, to undertake further development of the NSFnet. This relationship proved most fruitful. During the first several years of Merit's NSFnet operations, network traffic (measured in the number of packets routed) increased by roughly twenty percent per month.

With this dismantling of the ARPAnet, the NSFnet began to play a more important role as a national research network, and the Internet as we know it today began to emerge. Another role the emerging NSFnet began to assume was that of network "backbone" to the Internet.[1] However, in more recent years, as other service providers have begun to assume responsibility for development and maintenance of wideband services in the Internet, the NSF has attempted to downplay its role as Internet backbone provider in favor of its original supercomputer mission.

The Three-Tiered Network

When the NSF was seeking a partner to develop and expand the NSFnet, the network architecture was envisioned to have three distinct physical layers:

1. A *national network*, designed to connect the NSF-funded supercomputer centers and a series of regional networks using a wide bandwidth backbone;
2. A series of *intermediate or mid-level networks*, with regional (or disciplinary) networks centered roughly around the NSF supercomputer sites; and
3. *Local or campus networks*, allowing universities and commercial research centers to connect to the mid-level networks.

In reality, what has emerged in the Internet is a much more complex interrelationship of networks. In some locations, campus networks have emerged containing many distinct layers where Merit and the NSF envisioned a single bottom layer. Also, in addition to discipline-based and geographically centered mid-level networks, some networks of a political and/or administrative nature have emerged in the central layer of the model. For example, the state of New York operates its own state education and research network, in addition to the NSF mid-level regional centered around the Cornell Center for Theory and Simulation in Science and Engineering.

In addition to these tiers, an increasing number of distinct networks, many of them commercial networks such as The World and CompuServe, are beginning to develop or have developed "gateways" or "bridges" to the Internet. These gateways allow data (usually electronic mail) to be passed between the remote network and the many networks that comprise the Internet. It is sometimes difficult for the casual user to determine where the boundaries between these networks lie. In fact, sometimes even network veterans fail to understand the complex relationships that allow this emerging global data network to thrive. In Chapter Two, we examine these different network types and their inter-relationships in more detail.

The Proposed NREN

During the 101st session of the U.S. Congress, Senator Albert Gore (D-Tennessee) introduced the High Performance Computing Act (HPCA) of 1990 [S. 1067]. This bill was drafted to authorize Congress to appropriate funds to greatly expand the portion of the existing network directly attributable to the Federal Government—specifically, the NSFnet, the Department of Energy Network, and the few remaining pieces of the ARPAnet—into a network to be named the National Research and Education Network (NREN). The NREN legislation, designed to develop a high-performance network to serve the research needs of scientists throughout the United States, passed from the Senate Commerce, Science and Transportation Committee late in the 101st session. However, the House of Representatives failed to act on the bill before the 101st Congress adjourned, and the bill died.

Although the HPCA 1990 never came to a vote, it did lead the way for the High Performance Computing Act of 1991. This bill, S. 272, introduced by Senator Gore and eighteen cosponsors, closely resembled the compromise bill of the preceding Congressional term. However, several other similar bills were also introduced near the beginning of the 102nd Congress. Senator Bennett Johnston (D-Louisiana) introduced S. 343, the Department of Energy's version of the HPCA, and Representative George Brown (D-California) introduced H. 656, a bill similar to the S. 272, in the House of Representatives.

H. 656 was passed by the House of Representatives on July 11, 1991, and the two bills in the Senate were merged into a compromise bill at around the same time. With increased bipartisan sponsorship, this compromise bill passed the Senate by unanimous vote on September 11, 1991. In November 1991 the compromised version of the High Performance Computing Act of 1991 passed both the House and the Senate, and President George Bush signed the bill into law on December 9, 1991.

Although the legislation has been signed into law, it is important to note that the Federal Government has not appropriated any funds for the actual construction of the NREN. The HPCA bill authorized Congress to fund the project; however, to date, no funds have been forthcoming. Nevertheless, the development of the NREN has received strong bipartisan support throughout the Federal Government in the past, and it seems likely that funds for at least some parts of the project will be appropriated.

The Federal Networking Council

In 1990, in response to S. 1067 (the initial legislation introduced by Senator Gore), the Office of Science and Technology Policy (an executive branch agency) sponsored the creation of the Federal Networking Council (FNC). The FNC was formed to provide policy direction for the proposed NREN, and to coordinate the activities of various U.S. government agencies already operating high-performance computing networks. The Defense Advanced Research Projects Agency, the National Science Foundation, the National Aeronautics and Space Administration, and the Department of Energy, are among those agencies represented in the FNC. Its chair is Dr. Charles Brownstein of the National Science Foundation.

Although the High Performance Computing Act of 1991 is law, there were several issues which remained unresolved in Congress. Congress deferred decisions on these issues to the Executive Branch. One of the major issues left unresolved in the HPCA pertained to the question of administration of the network. It stands to reason that the agency named to lead the development of the NREN would benefit from an increased budget and new program responsibilities. For this reason, several of the agencies on the FNC were interested in being named the lead agency in the development of the NREN. The President has chosen the NSF to lead the development effort.

The Interim-Interagency NREN

On occasion, the term Interim-Interagency NREN will appear in writing or in presentations related to the NREN. This term has been used by the NSF to describe a period of time during which the existing Internet will migrate to what is envisioned to be the "full-fledged" NREN. This term is not used in this book; instead, our references to the emerging Federal network will all use the term "Internet."

The Evolution of a Network

In this chapter, we have given you a very brief historical view of the Internet, and have alluded to the rapid changes occurring in the network community. As a new network user, you may not fully understand the rapid changes that have occurred in the network; however, those familiar with the TCP/IP Internet are well aware of the changes involved. In Chapter Six we will return to some of the concepts and issues related to the rapid evolution of the network, but the better part of this book is dedicated to practical information that you, as a new network user, can employ. In the next chapter, we provide an overview of some of the current computer networks that make up the Internet or are linked to the Internet in the emerging global data network.

Note

1. The largest communications channel, with the highest capacity for data transmission (i.e., "bandwidth"), on a network is referred to as the network backbone.

Chapter Two: Overview of Current Networks

The number of telecommunications networks and networked computers available to students and scholars grows daily,[1] and it has become impossible to list or describe the networks that exist without including information that has become outdated. However, we have tried to give a brief overview of some of the major networks that make up the current Internet and the proposed National Research and Education Network (NREN). Some networks that are not part of the Internet itself, but have "gateways" that provide the ability to send electronic mail to and from Internet addresses, are also included.

This chapter looks first at some of the major players in the current Internet; the NSFnet backbone and the mid-level regional networks. It goes on to describe some cooperative networks, in which the participating sites are responsible for both financing and coordinating network use. Finally, it covers some commercial vendors providing access to both Internet gateways and the Internet itself.

Keep in mind that the information on these networks quickly becomes outdated. An updated list of Internet providers, including most of the networks described in this chapter, is available from the NSFnet Network Service Center (NNSC). To obtain the list, contact them at:

>NSF Network Service Center (NNSC)
>BBN Laboratories Inc.
>10 Moulton St.
>Cambridge, MA 02238
>(617) 873-3361
>nnsc@nnsc.nsf.net

The list can also be obtained through an automatic electronic mail utility. To request the list via electronic mail, send an e-mail message to:

```
info-server@nnsc.nsf.net
```

with the following text in the body:

```
request: nsfnet
topic: referral-list
request: end
```

Internet

The Internet, as explained in Chapter One, is a blanket term for a loose collection of networks. Some of the major networks making up the current Internet are described below.

DDN (Defense Data Network)

The (DDN) is a worldwide communications network serving the U.S. Department of Defense.

The DDN Network Information Center (NIC) assists current and potential subscribers in obtaining information about the DDN and the Internet. One of the better-known services provided by the DDN NIC is the WHOIS registry of users, hosts, domains, and networks. (The WHOIS program is described in the "E-Mail" section of Chapter Four.)

The NIC serves as a source of DDN documents, as well as the complete Internet Request for Comments (RFC) series and index (more information on RFCs is provided in Chapter Five). It also maintains an archive of information files, which are available for anonymous FTP and, in most cases, are accessible via the automatic mail server SERVICE@NIC.DDN.MIL.

The NIC also makes information from the Internet Engineering Tas force (IETF) available for FTP in the publicly accessible IETF: and INTERNET-DRAFTS: directories.

    Address: SRI International
                Network Information Systems Center
                Room EJ291
                333 Ravenswood Avenue
                Menlo Park, CA 94015
    E-mail: nic@noc.ddn.mil
    FTP site: nic.ddn.mil (192.67.67.20)
    Phone: (800) 235-3155 or (415) 859-3695

ESnet (Energy Sciences Network)

The ESnet is a nation-wide computer data communications network managed and funded by the U.S. Department of Energy Office of Energy Research (DOE/OER) for the purpose of supporting multiple program, open scientific research. ESnet is intended to facilitate remote access to major Energy Research (ER) scientific facilities, provide needed information dissemination among scientific collaborators throughout all ER programs, and provide widespread access to existing ER supercomputer facilities.

ESnet has connections to many of the mid-level regional networks, and to a number of other governmental and commercial networks on the Internet.

ESnet is installed and operated by the National Energy Supercomputer Center (NERSC), formerly known as the National Magnetic Fusion Energy Computer Center (NMFECC), which is located at Lawrence Livermore National Laboratory in California. NERSC provides user services for ESnet.

    Address: National Energy Research Supercomputer Center
                Lawrence Livermore National Laboratory
                P.O. Box 5509, L-561
                Livermore, CA 94551

E-mail: info@es.net
FTP site: nic.es.net (128.55.32.3)
Phone: (800) 33-ESNET

NSI (NASA Science Internet)

The NSI supports scientists and flight projects funded by NASA's Office of Space Science and Applications (OSSA). Users include NASA sites, and government facilities, research, and academic sites conducting NASA-funded research. The NSI is a NASA-wide network with hubs at several NASA centers.

Address: Network Information Center
          NASA Science Network
          MS 233-18
          NASA Ames Research Center
          Moffett Field, CA 94035
E-mail: nsnnic@nsipo.nasa.gov
Phone: (415) 694-5859 or (FTS) 464-5859

NSFnet/Merit

The National Science Foundation Network (NSFnet) is the backbone network of the U.S. National Science Foundation (NSF). It interconnects mid-level networks and other resources throughout the United States. The network may be used by researchers in general, according to NSF guidelines.

The NSFnet is managed by a group of five organizations—the NSF, IBM, MCI, Advanced Network and Services, and the Merit Network, Inc.

The Merit Network is a non-profit corporation owned and operated by nine of Michigan's four-year publicly supported universities. Merit also administers MichNet, a mid-level regional network in Michigan.

Address: MERIT Network, Inc.
          2901 Hubbard Drive
          ITI
          Ann Arbor, MI 48109-2112
E-mail: nsfnet-info@merit.edu
FTP site: nic.merit.edu (35.1.1.48)
Phone: (313) 936-3000

The NSF Network Service Center provides information services and technical assistance to NSFnet end-users. Information and documents (available online or printed) cover topics such as resources (the Internet Resource Guide), contacts at the mid-level networks and at local campuses and institutions (the Internet Managers' Phone Book), and network status reports. When prospective or current users do not know who to call concerning their questions about NSFnet use, they should contact the NNSC by electronic mail at nnsc@nnsc.nsf.net or by telephone at (617) 873-3400.

>Address: NNSC
>Bolt Beranek and Newman Inc.
>10 Moulton St.
>Cambridge, MA 02138
>E-mail: nnsc@nnsc.nsf.net
>FTP site: nnsc.nsf.net
>Phone: (617) 873-3400

Mid-level Regionals

The NSFnet includes a number of networks known as mid-level regionals. These networks provide inter-networking services to educational and commercial organizations in specific regional areas. Some of the larger mid-level regional networks are described below. (This information changes regularly, so some of this information may be out of date by the time this book is published.)

BARRnet (Bay Area Regional Research Network)

BARRnet was founded in 1986 by a consortium including the University of California campuses at Berkeley, Davis, Santa Cruz, and San Francisco, Stanford University, and the NASA Ames Research Center at Moffett Field. An NSF grant provided the initial funding for BARRnet, which was one of several regionally based networks initiated close to that time as part of the National Strategic Computing Initiative effort to build a national research network. BARRnet's primary mission at that time was defined as providing state-of-the-art connectivity among major research institutions and organizations.

At this time BARRnet is operated by Stanford University, which was the official recipient of the original NSF grant to BARRnet. All BARRnet employees are technically employees of Stanford University, which provides space, employee benefits, procurement and accounting services, and other support necessary for BARRnet's operation. BARRnet is currently 100 percent funded by member fees, and reimburses Stanford for the cost of these support services.

>Address: Pine Hall, Rm. 115
>Stanford University
>Stanford, CA 94305-4122
>E-mail: info@nic.barrnet.net
>FTP site: nic.barrnet.net
>Phone: (415) 725-1790

CERFnet (California Education and Research Federation Network)

The CERFnet is a regional network that operates throughout California. CERFnet's stated purpose is "to advance science and education by assisting the interchange of information among research and educational institutions through high-speed data communications techniques."

CERFnet provides both dedicated connections and dial-up services to its subscribers. The dial-up service, known as Dial 'N CERF, is designed for organizations and individuals with low or short-term needs for network services. Users of this service must abide by the network's "acceptable use" policy, which conforms with the NSFnet policy of restricting commercial use of the network. For more information on Dial 'n CERF, contact the CERFnet staff at the e-mail address shown below, or by calling (619) 534-5087.

> Address: CERFnet
> P.O. Box 85608
> San Diego, CA 92186-9784
> E-mail: help@cerf.net
> FTP site: nic.cerf.net (192.102.249.3)
> Phone: (800) 876-2373

CICnet

CICnet is a regional network serving a seven-state region of the midwestern United States. It connects the members of the Big Ten and the University of Chicago, as well as corporate and nonprofit organizations.

> Address: CICnet, Inc.
> 2901 Hubbard Drive
> Ann Arbor, MI 48109
> E-mail: info@cic.net
> FTP site: nic.cic.net (192.131.22.2)
> Phone: (313) 998-6103
> Fax: (313) 998-6105

CONCERT (Communications for N.C. Education, Research, & Technology)

CONCERT is a private telecommunications network owned and operated by the Center for Communications at Microelectronics Center of North Carolina (MCNC). Network participants include universities, research institutions, graduate centers, nonprofit organizations, government laboratories, and industries in North Carolina.

CONCERT is actually two networks; one for video, one for data. Both are carried over private microwave facilities within the state.

One of the services provided by CONCERT is CONCERT-CONNECT, a program providing businesses with the opportunity to access the Internet via direct network connection (at 56 Kbps or T1 speeds), or by three dial-up modem services: Serial Line Internet Protocol (SLIP); individual UNIX accounts; and UUCP mail/news accounts.

MCNC currently provides a "clearinghouse" for WAIS (Wide Area Information Server; see the "Advanced Applications" section of Chapter Four for more details on WAIS). In this role, they seek to facilitate collection, classification, and distribution of WAIS-related research and development information and products. (The Center also participates directly in WAIS research and development.)

>   Address: Center for Communications—MCNC
>   P.O. Box 12889
>   3021 Cornwallis Road
>   Research Triangle Park, NC 27709-2889
>   E-mail: info@concert.net
>   Phone: (919) 248-1466
>   (919) 248-1999 (CONCERT-CONNECT)
>   Fax: (919) 248-1405

CSUnet (The California State University Network)

CSUnet supports educational institutions throughout the state of California. This state-funded network provides free network access to all California State University campuses; other educational institutions can obtain access to the network for the cost of providing the connection.

The network's staff provides training and documentation to campuses upon request, and sponsors system-wide training for users, technical staff, and university groups.

An archive of user documentation and public domain software is maintained by the NIC, at nic.csu.net (130.150.102.20). These files can be obtained via anonymous FTP.

CSUnet is connected to the NSFnet at its Palo Alto and San Diego sites. It is a participant in CARL (the Colorado Alliance of Research Libraries) and BITNET (which is described in the "Cooperative Networks" section of this chapter). There are interconnections with three other California regional networks, BARRnet, CERFnet, and SDSCnet. Direct access to Sprintnet, a public packet-switch network, is also provided.

>   Address: CSUnet User Services
>   California State University Chancellor's Office
>   P.O. Box 3842
>   Seal Beach, CA 90740-7842
>   E-mail: nethelp@calstate.edu
>   FTP site: nic.csu.net (130.150.102.20)
>   Phone: (310) 985-9661

JvNCnet (North East Research Regional Network)

JvNCnet connects research organizations concentrated in the Northeastern United States, with access to the NSFnet backbone and with international connections to several Scandinavian countries (Norway, Finland, Iceland, Sweden, and Denmark), and the United Kingdom.

JvNCnet maintains an archive of RFCs, which are described in more detail in Chapter Five. It also provides an e-mail service for sites unable to use FTP. Address the request to:

SENDRFC@JVNC.NET

In the subject field of the message indicate the RFC number in the form RFC *nnnn*, or *index*, for the latest RFC Index.

Address: JvNCnet
         Princeton University
         B6 von Neumann Hall
         Princeton, NJ 08544
E-mail: nisc@nisc.jvnc.net
FTP site: ftp.jvnc.net
         market@jvnc.net
Phone: (800) 35TIGER
         (609) 520-2000

Los Nettos

Los Nettos is a regional network in the Los Angeles area. It may be used for any educational or research purpose. Member organizations are universities and research laboratories. The Information Sciences Institute (ISI) of the University of Southern California (USC) acts as the agent for Los Nettos.

Address: Los Nettos
         c/o Ann Westine
         USC/Information Sciences Institute
         4676 Admiralty Way
         Marina del Rey, CA 90292
E-mail: los-nettos-request@isi.edu
Phone: (213) 822-1511

MichNet

MichNet is a statewide network operated by Merit. MichNet was originally called the Merit Network, and was administered by Merit Network, Inc. When Merit and its partners gained responsibility for the NSFnet administration, they changed the name of the Michigan network to MichNet to avoid confusion. The network plans to reach out beyond Merit's traditional audience of four-year, publicly supported colleges and universities in Michigan.

Address: MichNet (a project of Merit Network, Inc.)
         5115 IST Bldg.
         2200 Bonisteel Blvd.
         Ann Arbor, MI 48109-2099
E-mail: Info@merit.edu (Query for documents: nis-info@nic.merit.edu or
         NIS-INFO@MERIT.BITNET)
FTP site: nic.merit.edu (35.1.1.48)
Phone: (313) 764-9430

MIDnet

MIDnet is a regional computer network for the seven Midwestern states. The network provides researchers access to supercomputers and is a vehicle for exchanging information among researchers.

    Contact: Dale Finkelson
    E-mail: dmf@westie.unl.edu
    Phone: (402) 472-5032

MRnet (Minnesota Regional Network)

The MRnet is an NSF regional network which provides communications between the nationwide NSFnet and researchers at the Minnesota Supercomputer Center, the University of Minnesota, and other educational institutions. MRnet also provides NSFnet access to several Minnesota organizations involved in high-technology research.

    Address: Minnesota Regional Network
              511 11th Avenue South, Box 212
              Minneapolis, MN 55415
    E-mail: info@mr.net
    FTP site: nic.mr.net (137.192.240.5)
    Phone: (612) 342-2570
    Fax: (612) 344-1716

NCSAnet (National Center for Supercomputing Applications Network)

NCSAnet is a regional supercomputing network that connects university and government research sites primarily located in Illinois, Wisconsin, and Indiana. The NCSAnet private corporate network is national in scale.

    Address: NCSAnet
              Attn: Charlie Catlett
              National Center for Supercomputing Applications
              605 E. Springfield Ave.
              Champaign, IL 61820
    E-mail: network@ncsa.uiuc.edu
    Phone: (217) 244-8297 [NCSA Networking Office]

NEARnet (New England Academic & Research Network)

The NEARnet is a high-speed network of academic, industrial, government, and nonprofit organizations in New England.

    Address: NEARnet
              10 Moulton St.
              Cambridge, MA 02138
    E-mail: nearnet-staff@nic.near.net
    FTP site: nic.near.net (192.52.71.4)
    Phone: (617) 873-8730 [NEARnet hotline]

NevadaNet
NevadaNet is a state-wide network that currently serves the following institutions: Community College of Southern Nevada; Desert Research Institute; Northern Nevada Community College; Truckee Meadows Community College; University of Nevada, Las Vegas; University of Nevada, Reno; and Western Nevada Community College.

> Address: University and Community College System of Nevada
> System Computing Services
> 4505 Maryland Parkway
> Las Vegas, NV 89154
> E-mail: Zitter@nevada.edu
> Phone: (702) 784-6133 [Don Zitter]

NorthWestNet (Northwestern States Network)
NorthWestNet provides communication with NSFnet for research centers throughout the Northwest, including sites in Alaska, Idaho, Montana, North Dakota, Oregon, and Washington. Members include institutions of higher education, groups of higher education institutions, computer networks, public school districts, private and public elementary and secondary schools, business, government, and nonprofit organizations, and local, state and regional economic development groups.

> Address: Dan Jordt
> University Networks and Distributed Computing
> UW, HG-45
> 3737 Brooklyn Ave. NE
> Seattle, WA 98105
> E-mail: danj@cac.washington.edu
> Phone: (206) 543-7352

NYSERNet (New York State Education & Research Network)
NYSERNet, Inc. is a not-for-profit corporation whose mission is to advance science, technology, and education by providing access to information and encouraging collaboration among educational institutions, library services, hospitals, government agencies, and industries involved in education and research, through use of high-speed data computer networks.

NYSERNet provides educators and researchers: (1) the mechanisms and infrastructure for improved collaboration; (2) access to specialized databases and on-line libraries; (3) access to the NSFnet, DARPA, NASA, and DOE supercomputer and parallel processing facilities throughout the United States; (4) access to national networks; and (5) creative, state-of-the-art tools to facilitate these activities.

NYSERNet, Inc. offers a range of high-performance, reliable TCP/IP internetworking services to users of electronic information and cutting-edge computing resources through its primary networking services provider, Performance Systems International, Inc. (PSI). These services include hard-wired connections to the Internet; dial-up "on-demand" access to the Internet for individuals and local area networks; access to Usenet newsgroups; a local electronic mail service providing unlimited messaging for a flat monthly fee; and NYSERNet Library and K-12 Networking Interest Groups.

NYSERNet also sponsors user meetings and conferences, workshops and documentation on using the network, and an FTP site for general information on the NYSERNet network and the Internet as a whole.

Address: NYSERNet, Inc.
111 College Place
Syracuse, NY 13244-4100
E-mail: info@nysernet.org
FTP site: nysernet.org
Phone: (315) 443-4120
Fax: (315) 425-7518

OARnet (Ohio Academic Resources Network)
OARnet is the regional network for the state of Ohio. It serves the entire higher education community.

E-mail: alison@oar.net
Phone: (614) 292-9248

PREPnet (Pennsylvania Research and Economic Partnership Network)
PREPnet, a mid-level network serving Pennsylvania, is a partnership of major research universities, state government, and the regional Bell operating company, Bell Telephone of Pennsylvania. Current members include educational and research institutions, industrial firms, and government agencies.

Address: PREPnet
530 N. Neville Street
Pittsburgh, PA 15213
E-mail: prepnet+@andrew.cmu.edu
FTP site: ftp.pitt.edu (/prepnet directory)
Phone: (412) 268-7870

PSCnet (Pittsburgh Supercomputing Center Academic Affiliates Group Network)
PSCnet is an NSF supercomputing site which is part of a joint venture among Carnegie Mellon University, University of Pittsburgh, and Westinghouse. It provides supercomputing resources for education and industry on the Internet. PSCnet also provides connectivity to the Internet for all of Pennsylvania through the mid-level regional network PREPnet.

Address: The Pittsburgh Supercomputing Center
4400 Fifth Avenue
Pittsburgh, PA 15213

E-mail: pscnet-admin@psc.edu
Phone: (412) 268-4960

SDSCnet (San Diego Supercomputer Center Network)

SDSCnet is a network linking academic, industrial, and government affiliates with the San Diego Supercomputer Center (SDSC), which administers the network, and, by extension, NSFnet.

Address: Paul Love
          San Diego Supercomputer Center
          P.O. Box 85608
          San Diego, CA 92186-9784
E-mail: loveep@sds.sdsc.edu
Phone: (619)534-5000

Sesquinet (Texas Sesquicentennial Network)

Sesquinet is a regional network in Texas. Its members include universities, research laboratories, and industrial organizations

Address: Dept. of Computer Science
          Rice University
          Houston, TX 77251-1892
E-mail: farrell@rice.edu
Phone: (713) 527-4988 [Farrell Gerbode]

SURAnet (Southeastern Universities Research Network)

SURAnet is an NSFnet mid-level network. SURAnet's geographic area includes the District of Columbia and thirteen states in the Southeast United States: Alabama, Delaware, Florida, Georgia, Kentucky, Louisiana, Maryland, Mississippi, North Carolina, South Carolina, Tennessee, Virginia, and West Virginia. While SURA, the parent organization, is a consortium of academic organizations, SURAnet members comprise approximately two-thirds academic institutions and one-third non-academic sites.

Address: SURAnet
           8400 Baltimore Blvd.
           Suite 101
           College Park, MD 20740
E-mail: suranet-admin@noc.sura.net
FTP site: ftp.sura.net (128.167.254.179)
Phone: Administration: (301) 982-4600
           (NIC services; new installations; systems)
           Technical Services: (301) 982-3214
           (operations)

TENET (Texas Education Network)

TENET was established in late 1991 to serve as a communication system for the Texas K-12 educational system. TENET users gain access to the Internet via THEnet.

TENET allows educators and students to use a variety of Internet resources, including library catalogs, file archives, and public databases. In addition, TENET offers training courses, electronic conferencing, and electronic mail with gateways to other networks.

Address:	Connie Stout
	Texas Education Agency
	1701 N. Congress Ave.
	Austin, TX 78701
E-mail:	cstout@tenet.edu
Phone:	(512) 463-9091 [voice]
	(512) 463-0828 ex. 39091 [voice mail]
Fax:	(512) 463-9090

THEnet (the Texas Higher Education Network)

THEnet is an NSFnet regional network that covers the state of Texas, with a link to the Instituto Tecnologico y de Estudios Superiores de Monterrey in Monterrey, Mexico. Network information and operations management are provided through the University of Texas (UT) System Office of Telecommunication Services (OTS).

Address:	Texas Higher Education Network Information Center
	University of Texas System
	Office of Telecommunication Services
	Service Building, Room 319
	Austin, TX 78712-1024
E-mail:	BITNET: INFO@THENIC
Internet:	info@nic.the.net
Phone:	(512) 471-2444
Fax:	(512) 471-2449

VERnet (Virginia Education and Research Network)

VERnet is the regional network for the state of Virginia.

Address:	VERnet (The Virginia Education and Research Network)
	Academic Computing Center
	Gilmer Hall
	University of Virginia
	Charlottesville, VA 22903
E-mail:	jaj@virginia.edu
FTP site:	ftp.ver.net (128.143.2.7)
	cd to directory ver_net
Phone:	(804) 924-0616

Westnet (Southwestern States Network)

Westnet is a regional network with nodes in Arizona, Colorado, southern Idaho, New Mexico, Utah, and Wyoming. Member organizations are universities and state networks. The state networks connect research laboratories, educational institutions, and commercial organizations.

WiscNet

WiscNet is a high-speed regional network providing access to network resources for higher educational institutions in the state of Wisconsin. It links Wisconsin institutions to regional, national, and international computer networks, including BITNET and the Internet networks. WiscNet itself provides no direct services to end-users; its primary purpose is to provide Internet access to its member institutions. The network is connected to the CICnet regional network, which is also described in this chapter.

> Address: Network Information Center MACC
> 1210 W. Dayton St.
> Madison, WI 53706
> E-mail: wn-info@nic.wiscnet.net
> FTP site: nic.wiscnet.net
> Phone: (608) 262-9421
> (608) 262-6886

Terrestrial Wideband Network

The Terrestrial Wideband Network supports research in high-speed networking, provides connectivity among academic and government sites, and supports a test-bed for Internet protocol development and experimentation with applications. It supports a research environment for multimedia conferencing and voice/video conferencing using gateways which use a real-time connection-oriented protocol over a connectionless network.

> Address: Terrestrial Wideband Network
> c/o BBN Systems and Technologies
> 10 Moulton St.
> Cambridge, MA 02138
> E-mail: wbhelp@bbn.com
> Phone: (617) 873-3427 (Terrestrial Wideband Network hotline)

Cooperative Networks

The term "cooperative networks" refers to networks in which the individuals and organizations making up the network administer and support the costs of the network through cooperative activities, rather than through centralized agencies such as the NSF. These networks are generally administered by a non-profit organization or council made up of representatives from the participating sites.

BITNET

BITNET (the Because It's There Network, or, alternatively, the Because It's Time Network) is a cooperative network composed primarily of mainframe computers at academic institutions in the United States. The BITNET network was started in 1981, with a link between the computers at Yale University and the City University of New York. It took less than two years for the network to stretch as far as California, and to include twenty schools. Since then, it has grown to include hundreds of sites, and thousands of host computers worldwide.

The network was designed to be unrestrictive and inexpensive; during its first years, the only requirements of a new site were that they pay for their own leased line connection to another BITNET site, and that they agree to serve as a connection point for at least one other participating institution. A membership fee, based on the institution's total annual budget, is now charged to new BITNET members. Revenues from these fees are used to fund support services.

Because BITNET was based on IBM mainframe technology (IBM's RSCS, or Remote Spooling Communications Subsystem), participation was at first limited to universities with IBM or IBM-compatible computers. Software has since been developed to emulate RSCS on other operating system environments; this has enabled a number of non-IBM hosts to join the network.

BITNET is a store-and-forward network that primarily supports transfer of files (like electronic mail and file transfer), rather than services that require an instant response (like Telnet). The data rates supported are much slower than those on the NSFnet, and there are no redundant paths for data; only one path exists between any two hosts.

Several gateways exist to exchange mail between BITNET and the Internet. In addition, many BITNET sites are also on the Internet, by virtue of their participation in a mid-level regional network. For example, the University of Alabama is both a BITNET node (UA1VM) and an Internet site (ua1vm.ua.edu). This can cause confusion for users at dual sites, since a BITNET address alone (USER@NODE) is not sufficient for an Internet address.

To use the BITNET/Internet gateway, an Internet user must address the mail to USER@NODE.BITNET.

FidoNet

FidoNet is a loose coalition of microcomputer-based bulletin board systems (bbs) which are capable of exchanging messages. Originally, the participating systems used Fido software, which explains the network's name. Over time, however, a wide variety of bbs software packages have been modified or created to handle Fido protocols.

The network was begun in May 1984, by two bbs system operators ("sysops") who were experimenting with unattended file transfer. They wrote programs that allowed their computer systems to call each other during the night, when long-distance telephone costs were lowest, and users were least likely to be logged onto their systems. When this proved successful, they began encouraging other sysops to add their bbs to the network. By August 1984, there were thirty nodes; by September there were fifty. By February 1985, there were 160 systems, and a group of sysops in St. Louis had taken over the administration of the list of systems. The network now includes several thousand nodes worldwide.

The primary use of the FidoNet network is to transmit messages in public conferences known as "echoes." Echomail travels as individual mail messages, and is forwarded from one system to another over the course of several days. Some FidoNet systems also support NetMail, which is private e-mail transmitted over the network.

FidoNet is organized into geographical divisions of zones, regions, networks, and points. A zone is a very large division; zone 1 is North America, zone 2 is Europe, and zone 3 is Australia, New Zealand, etc. Large zones are then subdivided into regions, designated with two-digit numbers to differentiate them from zones and networks. For example, region 11 in North America includes Illinois, Indiana, Kentucky, Michigan, Ohio, and Wisconsin. Regions are assigned two-digit numbers to differentiate them from networks.

Each region is broken down into individual networks. A network generally covers a single metropolitan area. For example, the Washington, D.C. area is assigned network number 109.

Within networks, each individual bbs has its own node number, which can be a two- or a three-digit number. And to make things more complicated, each bbs can also support one-person systems, which are called "points." A point receives mail from a bbs system, but does not redistribute that mail.

FidoNet addresses are written in the form zone:net/node.point. For example, Elizabeth Lane's full FidoNet address is: 1:375/14.901. In this example, 1 refers to the North American zone, 375 to the Alabama region, 14 to the bbs system, and 901 to the individual point number.

There are gateways in place to pass mail between FidoNet and the UUCP/UUNet network. Internet users can send mail to FidoNet users (if the user's FidoNet node supports private NetMail) in the following format:

```
User.Name@f#.n#.z#.fidonet.org
```

where: f# is the bbs node number,
       n# is the regional network number, and
       z# is the zone number.

Address: International FidoNet Association (IFNA)
               P.O. Box 41143
               St. Louis, MO 63141

FrEdMail (Free Educational Mail)

Like FidoNet, the FrEdMail Network is an informal, grass-roots telecommunications network. Unlike FidoNet, it was initiated with a specific audience in mind:

students and teachers in K-12 schools. The over 120 nodes allow teachers to "share experiences with student assignments, distribute teaching materials and curriculum ideas, promote the development of effective reading and writing skills, and obtain information about workshops, job opportunities, legislation affecting education, and new nodes on the growing network.[2]

FrEdMail, like FidoNet, is made up of individual bulletin board systems (considered "nodes"). Each bbs is operated by an institution—ranging from a university to a county office of education—or by an individual teacher or administrator in a school office, classroom, or even private home. Since each node is individually administered, it can provide services that are custom-tailored to local needs. Because ownership is local, it often is subsidized by public funding, and therefore allows free access to the network for local users.

Recently, FrEdMail instituted a prototype gateway to the CERFnet mid-level regional network in California. This gateway, based on a Usenet (see entry for Usenet in this chapter) model of conferences and "news feeds," provides access for FrEdMail users to other network participants across the country and even overseas. This type of link between locally operated systems and the international networking community may well serve as a model for future K-12 participation in the NREN.

For more information on FrEdMail, contact Al Rogers, executive director, by electronic mail at alrogers@cerf.net or send a message to help@cerf.net.

Free-Nets

The Free-Net concept was originated by Dr. Tom Grundner of Case Western Reserve University in Cleveland, Ohio. Dr. Grundner began with a bulletin board system (bbs) intended to provide health care information to the community. His bbs attracted corporate, governmental, and university sponsorship. It grew into a large-scale community information system providing electronic mail, conferencing, and a variety of information resources to the citizens of Cleveland and the surrounding Northeastern Ohio area. The Cleveland Free-Net is now one of four Free-Nets operating in Ohio.

From the original Cleveland Free-Net project, a coordinating group called the National Public Telecomputing Network (NPTN) has sprung up, also headed by Dr. Grundner. The NPTN plays a role similar to that of the National Public Radio (NPR) or the Public Broadcasting System (PBS); it organizes, connects, and pipes reference material to Free-Nets.

Many cities and states are beginning Free-Nets of their own as a result of the success of this community-access computing experiment. The following cities have developed formal organizing committees and are currently in the process of bringing Free-Net community computer systems online (this was the most recent information available from the NPTN as of the writing of this book; an updated list can be obtained by contacting the NPTN or by connecting to an existing Free-Net and reading the list online):

Buffalo Free-Net Organizing Committee
    James Finamore
    Director of Job Training
    Town of Tonawanda
    1835 Sheridan Drive
    Buffalo, NY 14223
    (716) 877-8165

Chicago Free-Net Organizing Committee
    Paul Bernstein, J.D.
    333 East Ohio Street #2102B
    Chicago, IL 60611-3033
    (312) 951-8451

Denver Free-Net Organizing Committee
    Diane Skiva, Ph.D
    Campus Box C-288
    4200 E. 9th Ave.
    Denver, CO 80262
    (303-270-8665

Helsinki Vapaa-Verkko Organizing Committee
    Paivi Hyvarinen
    User Services Section, Room U249
    Computing Center, Helsinki University of Technology
    Ostakaari 1 M
    SF-02150 Espoo, Finland
    358 + 0 - 451 4316

Lorain County Free-Net Organizing Committee
    Steven W. Leslie, M.D.
    St. Joseph Medical Office Building
    221 West 21st Street
    Lorain, OH 44052
    (216) 246-4000

Minneapolis/St. Paul Free-Net Organizing Committee
    Wallys Conhaim
    Conhaim Associates, Inc.
    2566 West Lake of the Isles Blvd.

Minneapolis, MN 55405
    (612) 374-9455

Oregon Free-Net Organizing Committee
    Jim Williams
    9845 S.W. Ventura Court
    Portland, OR 97223
    (503) 494-6059

Philadelphia Free-Net Organizing Committee
    Lance Simpson, Ph.D.
    Jefferson Medical College
    Room 314 JAH
    1020 Locust Street
    Philadelphia, PA 19107-6799
    (215) 955-8381

Summit Free-Net Organizing Committee
    Beth Kinney
    140 Ashland Road
    Summit, NJ 07901
    (908) 273-0320

Tuscaloosa Free-Net Organizing Committee
    Ron Doctor
    University of Alabama
    School of Library and Information Studies
    513 Main Library
    Tuscaloosa, AL

Washington Free-Net Coalition
    Terry Miller and Rhona Saunders
    3707 Military Road
    Washington D.C. 20015
    (202) 833-9550 (Rhona Saunders)

Wellington Free-Net Organizing Committee
    Manager, Computer Services
    Wellington City Council
    P.O. Box 2199
    Wellington, New Zealand
    +64 4 801-3300

Internet users who would like to explore the Cleveland Free-Net as visitors or obtain accounts may Telnet to the following addresses:

> freenet-in-a.cwru.edu
> freenet-in-b.cwru.edu
> freenet-in-c.cwru.edu

Those not having Telnet access may dial direct to (216) 368-3888 which supports 2400 baud 8N1. (Although there are 64 dial-up lines, the 25,000 users of the system keep those busy much of the time.)

Network users can obtain information on the Free-Nets via FTP from nptn.org (192.55.234.52), or by sending an e-mail message to info@nptn.org.

Dr. Grundner, the developer of the Cleveland Free-Net, the National Public Telecomputing Network, and the concept of Free-Net community computing, can be reached at the following address:

> T.M. Grundner, Ed.D., Director
> The Community Telecomputing Laboratory
> Case Western Reserve University
> 319 Wickenden Building
> Cleveland, OH 44106
> (216) 368-5121

K12net

K12net is a decentralized network of bulletin board systems throughout North America, Australia, Europe, and the Commonwealth of Independent Sates (formerly the USSR). The network is based on FidoNet technology, and allows students and educators to share curriculum-related conferences at no cost. Like FidoNet, K12net has conferences that are referred to as "echoes." These conferences, in addition to being distributed by the individual organizations participating in K12net, are now also being sent to selected Usenet and FidoNet sites.

K12net provides millions of teachers, students, and parents in metropolitan and rural areas worldwide with the ability to meet and talk with each other, to discuss educational issues, to exchange information, and to share resources on a global scale.

Unlike other school-oriented networks, K12net's explosive growth since its founding in September 1990, can be attributed to several factors which make it separate and distinct:

1. K12net provides students, teachers, and community members with access to free international telecommunications capabilities with an educational orientation on a local call. This frees up classroom, student, and home budgets for other things.
2. It is relatively easy and inexpensive to set up a K12net bbs. The only equipment required is an MS-DOS or Macintosh computer, modem,

and phone line. System software is very low in cost (if not free) and technical operation skills are developed in-house. Students may act as system operators.

3. It is decentralized. Each participating bbs is locally owned, controlled, and operated. It can be oriented to serve the needs of the local school and is an excellent vehicle for developing community relations.
4. It is an excellent vehicle for providing students, teachers, and parents with a gentle introduction to global telecommunications as a classroom tool—promoting literacy, a global perspective, and competency in up-to-date information technologies.

For more information, contact:

Address: Janet Murray, Wilson High School
1151 S.W. Vermont St.
Portland, OR 97219
Phone: (503) 280-5280
K12net: 1:105/23 (503/245-4961)
Internet: jmurray@psg.com

Usenet/UUNET

The term "Usenet" is often used to describe a network, an organization, and a service. In strict terms, however, it is only a service. Usenet is a conferencing system, which consists of a hierarchy of discussion groups known as "newsgroups." Individual messages posted to a newsgroup are called "articles."

Usenet newsgroups cover a broad range of topics, ranging from astrology to Zenith computers. At present, there are over 600 newsgroups, and the number continues to grow. The newsgroup structure is discussed at greater length in Chapter Four, in the "Mailing Lists/Electronic Conferences" section.

Usenet is often confused with UUNET, which is a non-profit communications service designed to provide access to Usenet news, mail, and various source archives at low cost by obtaining volume discounts. Charges are calculated to recover costs from participating organizations.

When Usenet was first established, it used a protocol known as UUCP, over long-distance dial-up lines, to transmit newsgroup messages. At that time, distribution was controlled by a few well-connected academic sites. In recent years, however, as the number of Internet sites has expanded, and the cost of long-distance calls has dropped, it has become possible for even small sites in the United States to obtain Usenet feeds. (In Europe, access to Usenet feeds has been more strictly controlled by more hierarchical organizations with central registries.)

For more information on UUNET, send your postal mail address to info@uunet.uu.net (uunet!info).

Commercial Information Exchange (CIX)

In 1991, the Commercial Internet Association (CIX) was formed as a trade association open to all commercial internet TCP/IP network providers/carriers.

The primary goal of CIX is to provide connectivity among cooperating TCP/IP carriers, with no restrictions on the commercial use of the network (in contrast to the NSFnet "acceptable use" policy, which restricts commercial use of the NSFnet backbone network).

As of February 1992, the following organizations and networks were members of CIX: BARRnet; CERFnet; Performance Systems International (PSI); UUNET Technologies; and U.S. Sprint.

Getting Access

Although many librarians, educators, and researchers already have access to the Internet through their institutional affiliations, there are many more who do not. This section describes some of the options for Internet access that are available to individuals and small organizations.

Several of the networks described in the previous section provide accounts for individuals and small organizations. Contact the mid-level regional in your area to find out if they provide access to the public. CERFnet, CONCERT, JvNCnet, MichNet, NEARnet, and OARnet all provide public access services (for a fee); some other mid-level regionals may have implemented similar services.

The Free-Net concept (see "Cooperative Networks" in this chapter) is being implemented in a number of cities, and promises to bring Internet connectivity to a much broader spectrum of participants. If a Free-Net exists in your area, this may be an ideal place for you to begin your exploration of the Internet.

Another of the cooperative networks, FidoNet, provides users with the capability to send mail to and from the Internet through a gateway (see "Varying Levels of Network Connectivity" in Chapter Three). This can be an effective low-cost option for individuals to take advantage of electronic mail communications, and to participate in mailing lists and discussion groups.

A list of Internet service providers providing public access to the Internet is available via electronic mail or by file transfer over the Internet (FTP). The list, called PDIAL, can be requested via electronic mail by sending a message to kaminski@netcom.com with the text Send PDIAL in the subject line.

Some of the options for obtaining Internet access are described below.

Commercial Internet Providers

The price information for the services described below was current as of the writing of this book. However, prices are likely to fluctuate, and the information provided here should serve only as a general guideline for prices. For specific information on current prices, contact the service provider directly.

AlterNet

AlterNet, a public TCP/IP network service run by UUNET, offers Internet connections to organizations and individuals, regardless of their affiliation. UUNET provides dial-up and leased line UUCP and TCP/IP services, Usenet news feeds, and Domain Name registration. Their services are geared primarily toward group sites (bulletin board systems and other organizations) rather than individuals.

AlterNet provides connections to many other networks including several NSFnet mid-level regional networks, CIX, and PSInet. For organizations meeting NSF appropriate use qualifications, NSFnet access is provided at no extra charge.

> Address: 3110 Fairview Park Drive, Suite 570
>   Falls Church, VA 22042
>
> E-mail: alternet-info@uunet.uu.net
> Phone: (800) 4UUNET3
>   (703) 204-8000
> Fax: (703) 204 8001

ANS CO+RE

Advanced Network & Services (ANS) is a U.S.-based network service provider that offers connections to the Internet at a variety of bandwidth levels, including 56Kb/s, T1, 10Mb/s and T3. Currently, ANS has the only public T3 (45Mb/s) TCP/IP backbone networks in the world. ANS provides Internet connections for research and education institutions and government agencies. Through their wholly owned subsidiary, ANS CO+RE, these services are available to commercial organizations, including other network and information service providers. The network's operations center, located in Ann Arbor, Michigan, provides network operations services around the clock.

All research and education institutions and government agencies that have signed the ANS acceptable use policy as part of their contractual agreements with ANS are free to use the company's network to send and receive information related to research and education. Any commercial organization that has signed the ANS CO+RE acceptable use policy and the appropriate agreements for sending and receiving information that is commercial in nature (that is, not related to or in support of research and education) may use the ANS network. However, commercial traffic may not be sent through the network to any other network that does not allow commercial traffic to be carried across its gateways.

In addition to providing attachment services and the equipment for these connections, ANS offers the InterLock Security Service, which limits access between the Internet and private networks. It also offers consultation in the integration of high-speed networking into strategic planning, assistance in network engineering and design, and educational seminars in high-speed networking.

> Address: Advanced Network & Services, Inc.
>   100 Clearbrook Road
>   Elmsford, NY 10523
> E-mail: info@ans.net

Phone: (914) 789-5300
Fax: (914) 789-5310

Anterior Technology

Anterior Technology is a value-added computer communications services provider connected to BARRnet and to PSInet. Anterior is dedicated to full subscriber service and to innovation in communications and information services for the network community.

Services provided include Internet e-mail, Usenet news distribution, an FTP archive retrieval server (AutoFTP), and ClariNet news distribution.

Address: P.O. Box 1206
           Menlo Park, CA 94026-1206
E-mail: info@radiomail.net
Phone: 415-328-5615
Fax: 415-322-1753

DMConnection

DMConnection is a low-cost alternative for UUCP mail exchange and news feeds. It currently sells UUCP and NEWS feeds to the general public, and is negotiating a direct Internet connection.

It specializes in Macintosh and VAX/VMS support of UUCP and NEWS, providing several very large mail-based file servers archiving most of the major source news groups. Information on the supported file servers can be retrieved by sending mail to fileserv@dmc.com with a body containing the single line: help.

With the advent of a direct Internet connection, it will also offer a mail-based FTP server as well as interactive accounts for FTP, Telnet, and bbs support.

Address: 267 Cox St.
           Hudson, MA 01749
E-mail: dmc$info@dmc.com, dmc@dmc.com, info@dmc.com
Phone: (508) 568-1618
Fax: (508) 562-1133

MSEN, Inc.

MSEN was formed to bring reasonably priced Internet connections to the general public. They currently sell dial-up IP and UUCP mail/Usenet news connections, and will be offering shell login/bbs accounts in 1992. They provide services to help find resources on the Internet, either by connecting to their system and searching their archives, or through their consulting services.

Address: Owen Medd <osm@msen.com>
           President, MSEN, Inc.
           628 Brooks Street
           Ann Arbor, MI 48103

E-mail: info@msen.com
Phone: (313) 741-1120

NETCOM

NETCOM provides a complete comprehensive dial-up computer and communications service with services such as:

- dial-up shell access (Telnet/ftp/irc)
- news/mail/domain services (flat fee)
- UUCP services (no time charges)
- low-cost SLIP/PPP Internet connections
- e-mail (elm, mail, mush with username@machine formats)
- netnews (two weeks of news and over 2,000 groups)
- news readers: rn, trn, nn, zn, tin, vnews, readnews, and more
- shell access (csh, ksh, sh, tcsh, bash)
- compilers (c, gcc, g++, lisp, prolog, clips)
- over 200 custom utilities
- access with a local phone call from many California cities

E-mail: info@netcom.com
Phone: (408) 554-UNIX
Fax: (408) 241-9145

PSI (Performance Systems International)

PSI provides commercial Internet access to individuals and organizations, with varying levels of connectivity ranging from dial-up access to dedicated high-speed lines.

Their basic service for individuals is PSILink. Subscribers to this service receive software from PSI that allows off-line reading and responding to messages. As this book was being written, they had not yet made a Macintosh version of the software available, but they plan to release one in 1992.

In addition to electronic mail, PSI offers access to Usenet newsgroups, as well as use of an FTP server. The FTP server allows subscribers to submit a request for a file when its location is known. The server will fulfill the request and return the file to the user.

The current costs for PSILink are a $35 registration fee, $19/month for connect service at 2400 baud, $29/month for service at v.32, and $1 for every megabyte of files retrieved using FTP beyond a 50MB monthly allotment.

Address: Performance Systems International
           11800 Sunrise Valley Drive, Suite 1100
           Reston, VA 22091
E-mail: info@psi.com
Phone: (703) 620-6651
           (800) 82P-SI82

The World

The World is a relatively new public access UNIX™ system, being managed by the Boston-based Software Tool & Die company. It can be accessed by dialing directly to their local site, or by calling into any CompuServe local access number.

The basic rates are $2 an hour, twenty-four hours per day, and a $5 monthly account fee.

The 20/20 Plan is $20 paid in advance for twenty hours of online time during a one-month period. This includes the monthly account fee and an additional 1,500 blocks of disk space. After your first twenty hours, the hourly rate is $1 per hour.

Services provided include electronic mail (gatewayed to the Internet), Usenet newsgroups, electronic mailing lists on specific topics, an interactive "chat" function that allows users to interact with each other while logged onto the system, and a variety of UNIX™ software and utilities. Access to an Archie server (see Chapter Five) is also available, along with Telnet and FTP to some Internet and AlterNet sites.

To sign up for public access, use your modem to dial 617-739-WRLD. Alternatively, you can use the CompuServe Packet Network to connect. (To find your local access number, dial direct to CompuServe at 1-800-848-4480 using your modem. Enter the command "phones" at the prompt or call Software Tool & Die directly at 617-739-0202 and they will provide your local number.) After you have your local number, use your modem to dial it and enter "world,domestic" at the "Host name:" prompt. Use the password "notobvious" to gain access to The World.

At The World's login prompt, use the login "new" to begin the account request program. You will be asked a few questions necessary to create your account. VISA or MasterCard is accepted for billing purposes. The World will allow you to select your login name. Most people select their name, their initials, or a combination of both. Your login name will be your electronic mail address. Your initial password will be provided by the account creation software. For customers with credit cards, the account is available immediately upon completion of the request. Customers who request postal billing must contact Software Tool & Die's office for account activation.

Address: Software Tool & Die
          1330 Beacon Street
          Brookline, MA 02146
Phone: (617) 739-0202

Public Access UNIX Systems

Usenet and sometimes electronic mail access are available through a number of publicly accessible services. Some of these services are bulletin boards, while others are commercial services that offer services ranging from electronic mail and news feeds to databases and interactive games.

A list of public access Usenet sites is posted periodically on the alt.bbs.lists newsgroup. The December 1991 list is provided in the following table.

Column explanations
——————

Machine
————

Shorthand machine name. The full system name appears in the long
version. If the shorthand name is not part of the domain address,
you'll be referred to a note below.

Phone Number
——————

NEW USER telephone number. Systems with multiple lines will provide alternate numbers upon registration. Don't assume that the ne-
wuser line is 9600/v.32! Numbers are in North America unless pre-
ceded by a plus (+) sign.

Speeds
——————

Y = Yes; $ = Yes (with donation); V = Yes (upon verification);
F = (near) future addition

Column headings: a - 300; b - 1200; c - 2400, no MNP; d - 2400,
MNP4-5; e - 9600+, no MNP; f - 9600+ v.32/v.32bis; g - 9600+ HST;
h - 9600+ Hayes V-series; i - 9600+ Telebit PEP; j - other 9600+
(see long version)

Services
Y = Yes; $ = Yes (with donation); V = Yes (upon verification);
R = upon request; F = (near) future addition; X = Yes (with re-
strictions)

Column headings: a - Reading selected newsgroups; b - Posting to
selected newsgroups; c - Reading all newsgroups; d - Posting to
all newsgroups; e - Sending Email; f - Receiving Email; g - Mail
feed; h - News feed; i - Telnet; j - live FTP; k - batch FTP; l -
IRC; m - OS shell access

Other flags
($) ALL modem speeds and services require donation. If a service
on this site is marked with a "$", it requires an additional dona-
tion above the donation for access.
[x] See note #x below.

Machine	Phone Number	Speeds abcdefghij	Services abcdefghijklm	Other Flags	Location
abode	818-401-9666	-YY-----Y-	YYYYYYYY---YY	($)	El Monte CA
actrix	+4 389 5478	YYYYYY----	YYYYYYYYYY--Y	($)	Wellington NZE
aegis	+075-954-0118	-YYYYY----	YYYYYYYY----Y	($)	Kyoto JAP

Machine	Phone Number	Speeds abcdefghij	Services abcdefghijklm	Other Flags	Location
apres	708-639-8853	YYYY-YY---	---YYYYYY-----		Cary IL
arkham	604-983-3546	YYYYYY----	---YVYYYY-----		N Vancouver BC
bohemia	303-449-8946	YYYYYYY--Y	YYYYYY$$----Y		Boulder CO
chinet	312-283-0559	--Y$--$$$-	XXYYR-----Y		Chicago IL
clmqt	906-228-9460	YYY-------	$$$$$YYY----$		Marquette MI
ddsw1	312-248-0900	YYY--F--Y-	YY$$YY$$---$$		Chicago IL
dialix	+09 244 3233	YYY-------	Y$Y$$Y$$----Y	($)	Perth AUS
digex	301-220-0462	YYY-------	---YYYY-----Y	($)	Greenbelt MD
eclectic	none	YYYYYYYY--	YYYYYYYYYY--Y	($)[1]	Arlington MA
edsi	414-734-2499	--Y------F-	Y$$$$Y------R		Appleton WI
ersys	403-454-6093	YYYY-VY-V-	YVVVVYYY-----		Edmonton AB
gagme	312-714-8568	YYY--$----	YY$$YY$$--$-Y		Chicago IL
graphics	908-469-0049	YYYY---Y--	YYYYYY----Y--		Piscataway NJ
grebyn	703-281-7997	--Y-------	--YYYYYY--Y-Y	($)	northern VA
halcyon	206-292-9048	YYYY-Y--YY	YYYYYYY------		Seattle WA
halluc	703-425-5824	-YY-YYY---	--YVYYYY-----	($)	Fairfax VA
hogbbs	814-238-9633	YYYY------	YY---YYYY-----		StateCollege PA
infopls	708-537-0247	YYYYYY----	--YVYYYY-----		Wheeling IL
ixgch	+61 8115492	YYY---·---	YYYYYYYYY----Y	($)	Kaiseraugst SWI
kralizec	+2 837 1183	-YYYYY----	YYYYYY----Y-Y	($)	Sydney AUS
lakes	803-663-9819	YYYY----Y-	--YVVYYY-----		Aiken SC
loft386	none	YYYY----Y-	YYYYYY$$----Y	($)[2]	Rapid City SD
lunatix	606-278-8307	YYY------	YYYYYY$$----Y		Lexington KY
medsys	615-288-3957	-YY------Y-	YYYYYYRR-----		Kingsport TN
midnj	908-787-4541	YYY-------	Y$---$$-------		Middletown NJ
mpoint	718-899-0662	--Y---Y---	YYYYYYYY----Y	($)	Jackson Hts NY
nstar	219-289-0287	YYYYYYYYY-	--YYYYYYRRRRY	($)	South Bend IN
nysnet	518-484-1961	-YYYYY----	YYYYYYYY-----	($)	Albany NY
omo	+49 40873514	YYYYYYY---	--YYYY-------		Hamburg GER
oneb	604-753-9960	YYY-----Y-	YYY$$$$---$$R		Nanaimo BC
pain	818-776-1447	YYYYYY----	YYYYYYRR-----		Reseda CA
panix	718-832-1525	--YY----Y-	--YYYYR$FF-FY	($)	New York NY
pegasus	none	YYY-----Y-	--YYYYYY----Y	($)[3]	Honolulu HI
pro-haven	409-693-8262	YYYYYY----	YY-YYY-Y--R-Y		College Stn TX
pro-nbs	619-571-0152	-----Y----	--YYYYYY-----		San Diego CA
quack	408-249-9650	YYYY-Y--Y-	--YYYYY--Y-Y	($)	Santa Clara CA
rock	none	YYYYYYY-Y-	--YYYYYYYY-YY	($)[4]	North Carolina
sandv	708-352-0948	YYY-------	YY$$$YYY-----		LaGrange Pk IL
saviour	914-452-5538	YYYYYYY--Y	YYYYYY-------		Poughkeepsie NY
sdf	214-436-3281	YYY-------	YYYYYY-----Y		Dallas TX
spies	408-867-7790	YYY---Y--Y-	--YVYYYYYYYVV	[5]	Saratoga CA
sugar	713-684-5900	YYYYYY--Y-	YYYYYY$$$$$$-	[6]	Houston TX
techbook	503-644-8135	-YYYYY--Y-	--YYYY-----$		Beaverton OR
ttardis	313-350-2585	YYY-----Y-	--YYYYYY--Y-R		Southfield MI
unixland	508-655-3848	-YYYYYY-YY	YYYYYY$$----Y	($)	Natick MA

Machine	Phone Number	Speeds abcdefghij	Services abcdefghijklm	Other Flags	Location
vpnet	708-833-8126	YYYY----Y-	YY$$YYYY----$		Villa Park IL
vtcosy	703-232-9100	-YYY-----Y	Y-R-YY------	[7]	Blacksburg VA
wb3ffv	301-625-0817	-Y-Y-YY-Y-	YY----YY----R		Baltimore MD
world	617-739-9753	YYYYYY---Y-	--YYYYYYYYYY	($)	Boston MA
xenon	213-654-2822	YYYYYY---Y-	------YY----	($)	W Hollywood CA
zgnews	214-596-3720	YYYYYYY---	YYYYYYYR----		Dallas TX

=-=-=-=-=-=-=-=

Note 1 - Contact 617-643-3373 voice for access.
Note 2 - Contact 605-343-8760 voice for access.
Note 3 - Contact 808-735-5013 voice for access.
Note 4 - Rock Concert Net - net_address: rock.concert.net, Email
         to abc@rock.concert.net for access.
Note 5 - Spies in the Wire - net_address: apple.com
Note 6 - NeoSoft Comm Services - net_address: NeoSoft.com
Note 7 - Type CALL VTCOSY after connection to reach the site.

Commercial Service Mail Gateways

In addition to the networks described in the preceding sections, there are a number of commercial networks that, although they are not part of the Internet, provide their users with the ability to send e-mail to and from Internet users.

CompuServe

CompuServe is a commercial online service that provides access to databases, software libraries, conferences, online games, and electronic mail. Although most subscribers use the electronic mail to communicate with other CompuServe users, there is a gateway that allows the exchange of mail between CompuServe and Internet users.

Internet users can send a message to CompuServe users by addressing the message to: user.id@compuserve.com, where "user.id" is the CompuServe user id with a period substituted for a comma.

For example, for CompuServe id number 12345,6789, the address would be:

    12345.6789@compuserve.com

CompuServe users can send electronic mail to Internet users by following a specific addressing convention. In the "To:" field of the message, the preface >INTERNET: should appear, followed by the Internet address.

For example:

    To: >INTERNET: craig@cni.org

For more information about contacting CompuServe subscribers, try sending a message to the CompuServe postmaster, at the address: POSTMASTER-@COMPUSERVE.COM.

> Address: 5000 Arlington Center Boulevard
> Columbus, OH 43220
>
> Administrative: Neely, Sam (SN7)
> Contact: SAM@CSI.COMPUSERVE.COM
> (614) 457-8600
> Technical: Kleinpaste, Karl (KK53)
> Contact: karl@TUT.CIS.OHIO-STATE.EDU
> (614) 292-7347

MCI

The MCI Corporation, a well-known long-distance telephone carrier, also provides an electronic mail service with a gateway to the Internet.

Subscribers to the MCI Mail service have the ability to send messages to other MCI Mail users and to Internet users.

Interested readers can send requests for more information to the following address:

> MCI Mail
> 2000 M Street N.W.
> Washington, D.C. 20036

Notes

1. In the February '92 issue of MATRIX NEWS, in an article entitled "How Big is the Matrix?," John Quarterman estimates the current size of "the Internet" to be 727,000 hosts as of 1/92 with 3,650,000 users; he also estimate that the current rate of growth is approximately one new host per hour.
2. From the FrEdMail information release, available via anonymous from the CERFnet Network Information Center (nic.cerf.net).

Chapter Three: Technical Notes

Network users without technical or scientific backgrounds often ask "Why should I bother to learn the technical details of the Internet?" They may be more interested in a brief "cheat sheet" that will guide them through the execution of the specific tasks they need to complete. If they perform those tasks often enough, they will eventually discard the cheat sheet, knowing they have accomplished what they set out to learn. This is common among end-users of computer systems. The majority of end-users want to perform specific computing operations to aid them with their jobs, their research, and their personal interests; they often feel that "computing for the sake of computing," and all the technical details surrounding that activity, are best left to people in systems support groups.

Other end-users disagree with this philosophy. They see the development of technical self-sufficiency as a tool for life-long learning, and as a better goal in the training of computer users. Providing the user with a conceptual frame of reference is the only realistic way to teach people if you expect them to retain a basis of knowledge from which they can teach themselves. As end-users without formal technical training, but with a healthy level of technical knowledge gained from our experiences with computers, we hope to strike a balance between these two extremes in this book, and especially in this chapter.

Defining an appropriate level of technical expertise for librarians and educators to achieve (or, for that matter, defining a working definition of computer literacy for any professional) is a difficult task. This chapter will not attempt to define such educational criteria. Rather, it is intended to expose you to a selected set of the technical details underlying the tremendous technological infrastructure we call "the Internet." As this text is intended for relative newcomers to the network, the material in this chapter will only scratch the surface of the real inner workings of network operations, and suggest some additional sources for more detailed information on the topics included in this chapter. We do recognize, however, how difficult some of this information can be to obtain and process, even for those who are already using the Internet. As a result, it is likely that even those who consider themselves somewhat more than network novices will find some material in this chapter new or novel.

The Advent of the Network Age

An analogy often used among engineers and computer scientists is that it is not necessary to have a working knowledge of an internal combustion engine in order to drive an automobile. Similarly, it can be argued, it is not necessary to have a detailed working knowledge of your desktop computer, and the many layers of application software which inter-operate on the computer and the network, in order to achieve the moderate levels of productivity which most computer users desire.

Ultimately, this argument may prevail. However, for many reasons, it is premature to dismiss the need for any requisite knowledge of the relatively new area of networking technology. In the early days of development of many technologies, there is a critical period of rapid growth. During this period, many "amateurs" advance the state of the technology by openly embracing it and immersing themselves in its many aspects. We live in the day of the Internet "gentleman amateur."

Consider the following analogy: early in the twentieth century, before there was a national infrastructure of interstate highways, service stations, and roadside cafes, it would have been considered unwise to undertake a major trip without packing certain necessities. The list might include such items as water for the car's radiator, an extra can of gasoline, a small set of tools, an extra tire, and perhaps a picnic lunch. Similarly, the savvy network traveler of today collects comparable amenities to diagnose the inevitable barriers and overcome the minor obstacles which arise when navigating the byways of the networked world. Because network technology is still in such an early stage of development, there is a need—and, in fact, an opportunity—for those now connected to the Internet to achieve a basic level of understanding about the networked world which is evolving around them.

For managers, there is another compelling reason to gain a basic understanding of networking technology. In order to make informed and effective decisions regarding the purchase and maintenance of computing/networking hardware and software, it is necessary to understand something of the technology. While it is possible for a manager to rely on the advice of other "trusted" individuals, there is no substitute for a real understanding of the facts surrounding a decision, and the potential long-term ramifications of any decision being made.

Increasingly, the worlds of computing professionals and librarians are being drawn together. This is particularly evident in the field of higher education. There is a clear trend in academe toward bringing library and campus computing operations together under common administration. The rising cost of print materials, and the attractive, almost seductive, allure of electronic information processing are creating alliances where there formerly were none. A firm understanding of networking terminology provides a common language which can be shared between computing professionals and librarians. Because network growth is increasing so rapidly, neither librarians nor computer professionals can claim a monopoly in the delivery of electronic information. Both professions still have much to learn. Indeed, there is a growing interdependence between librarians and computer professionals in the network community. Such collaboration offers the best chance of achieving the vision of a truly ubiquitous information medium. For librarians and educators to learn the technology of networking fosters this collaboration, and will ultimately open career opportunities for those pioneers, as well as for those who follow.

The remainder of this chapter provides basic technical information to aid the network traveler. It would be impossible to provide enough information to solve all the potential problems. But the material within this chapter should provide a solid footing on which user self-sufficiency can be developed. The topics to be explored include: a general overview of packet-switching technology; an introduction to protocols (with particular attention to the Transmission Control Protocol/ Internet Protocol [TCP/IP] suite of protocols); concepts of network addressing;

file formats commonly encountered on the network; and, finally, varying levels of network connectivity and the effect the level of connection has on the services available to the user.

We assume that the reader has a basic understanding of computer operations (understanding such terms as bits, bytes, hardware, software, the operating system, and application software). Although there are many levels of networking technicalities (see "The Internetworking Protocols" section), a firm understanding of the "lower" technical layers of operations must be built on a firm foundation of computer operations.

Varying Levels of Network Connectivity

To use Internet applications and resources, you must have a connection to the Internet. This may appear as an overly simplistic statement, but there are several levels of increasingly complex connectivity to be considered. It is possible to be connected to a network without being connected to the Internet. And it is possible to be connected to the Internet, but not in such a way as to use all of the resources available on the network. Several different levels of network connectivity are examined below.

Phase Zero Connectivity: No Access to the Internet

With the tremendous amount of attention that the Internet has been receiving from librarians and educators alike, it is hard to believe that there are large numbers of people with no access to the network. And yet, the great majority of individuals who have access to computers, even in the research and education communities so well represented within the Internet, have a nonexistent level of connectivity to the Internet. If your computer is part of a local or wide area network that is not a part of the TCP/IP-based Internet, or has no "gateway" to send messages to or from Internet sites, you have no access to the applications or resources described in the following chapter. You may wish to refer back to Chapter Two, where many of the regional and commercial network service providers are discussed in more detail. There, you can identify an organization/network that can assist you in obtaining an Internet connection.

Phase One Connectivity: Gateway Access to the Internet

The first level of connectivity, and one of the easiest for individual users to obtain, is through a gateway from a smaller network to the Internet. Gateways are links between networks that allow for the interchange of data between the two networks. Generally, this data interchange is limited to the transmission of electronic mail, and possibly small files which can be shipped through a gateway using electronic mail protocols. Gateways normally do not allow access to Process/Application level protocol implementations such as Telnet and FTP (File Transmission Protocol).

However, the one exception to this rule entails information systems designed to receive input through a gateway, generally in the form of an electronic mail transmission, and can then parse the text of the message in order to receive and execute a command for a higher level process. One such service is Princeton's BITFTP gateway, which allows users on BITNET hosts to retrieve files via FTP from Internet hosts. A person on the BITNET can send an e-mail note to the BITFTP host at Princeton. The e-mail note must detail the Internet node, directory location, and the name of the file which one wants to retrieve. When BITFTP receives the note, it will initiate an FTP session, retrieve the file, and place it inside another e-mail note which is subsequently mailed back to the user. (See Chapter Four for more detailed information on the BITFTP gateway service.)

It is becoming increasingly common for cooperative and commercial networks to provide gateway access to the Internet. BITNET has several heavily-used gateways. MCI Mail and CompuServe both operate gateways between their networks and the Internet, as do FidoNet and K12net. The complexity of gateway operations vary. On some networks, including BITNET, the gateway process is invisible to the user; messages sent to an Internet e-mail address are automatically forwarded to the gateway site for routing to their recipient. On other networks, such as FidoNet or CompuServe, sending messages to Internet accounts requires special addressing conventions. The methods for using gateway access to the Internet vary substantially based on your host system; it is important to consult your system administrator or local system documentation to obtain instructions for your system.

More information on the technical aspects of gateways appears later in this chapter.

Phase Two Connectivity: Remote Access to the Internet

The second level of connectivity, quite common in academic environments, is through terminal access to a larger time-sharing host. If you use a "dumb" terminal, or communications software on a microcomputer that emulates a terminal, to log into a larger host computer (like an IBM mainframe or a VAX minicomputer), you are connected to the Internet at this level.

This level of access seems to offer people the greatest level of confusion regarding Internet services. The key to understanding the difference between this level of connectivity and Phase Three connectivity is to consider this question: "On what computer does the TCP/IP Process/Application protocol which I am executing reside?" The TCP/IP software resides on the larger time-sharing host, then you are connected to the network at level two. In this case, your access to TCP/IP applications is limited to those available on that host system. Most often, those applications are selected for use by a site administrator, and you will have seemingly little input regarding the implementation of those applications.

Another key question to ask yourself when you try to determine which level of connectivity you have is, "Do I have to use another serial protocol, such as Kermit or Xmodem, to download files to my desktop computer?" If you are able to use an application such as FTP to move files between remote hosts on the Internet and your local time-share host, but must use another serial file transfer protocol such as Kermit to upload and download between the time-share host and your workstation, then you are connected to the Internet at level two. TCP/IP, which runs the entire length of the network directly to the host on your desktop, entails connectivity at level three.

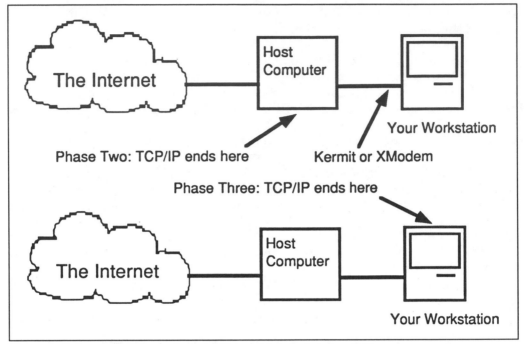

Figure 1. A diagram of phases two and three of Internet connectivity.

Phase Three Connectivity: Direct Access to the Internet

At level three connectivity, your local microcomputer or workstation is actually a host on the Internet. Rather than connecting as a terminal to a larger time-sharing host, you are directly connected to the Internet itself. Your desktop computer has its own assigned IP address.

With direct desktop connectivity, the number of applications available to you for use is greatly increased. It is important to note that the varying levels of connectivity are additive. That is, a person connected to the Internet at level three can also have access to all level one and level two applications. The main advantage of level three connectivity is the ability to utilize advanced client/server applications (discussed in Chapter Four). Additionally, to a large degree, you control the software applications used for network access—not a system administrator. Your disk storage space and processing power are only limited by the configuration of your desktop host.

Getting a direct connection to the Internet usually requires the assistance of a network administrator. At the very least, it requires a dedicated circuit to a mid-level service provider able to provide you with such services as name domain resolution. At a college or university, this assistance generally comes through a central computing center, although it is possible that certain large regions of the organization are administered elsewhere. For example, many university libraries operate their own sub-networks with the campus network infrastructure. If you are using a commercial service provider, or are working directly with another agency which is providing your network services, you should contact them about achieving level three connectivity.

Connectivity and Applications

Obviously your level of connectivity has a direct impact on which applications are available to you as a network user. This issue should become more clear as you continue through this book. In the rest of this chapter, as well as the chapters that follow, we have differentiated between remote applications for users with Phase One connectivity, host applications for users with Phase Two connectivity, and desktop applications for users with Phase Three connectivity.

An Introduction to Packet-Switching

The majority of librarians, educators, and researchers have had some exposure to serial computing communications. Over the last several decades, the use of terminal devices (originally teletype machines, followed by CRTs, and then by personal computers using terminal emulation software) among these individuals has become commonplace. Personal computers, modems, and remote databases are routinely used by the academic researcher. In particular, librarians have become familiar with this form of telecommunications through their work with remote on-line bibliographic databases (such as those marketed by BRS, DIALOG, and Dow Jones).

However, the Internet, which is based on the TCP/IP protocol suite, differs from the serial computer communications with which most librarians and researchers are familiar. The differences stem from the method used to exchange data between computers on the network—a method of data interchange known as packet-switching.

Serial computer communications are characterized by relatively slow data speeds (from 300 to 9,600 bits per second), a steady stream of analog data, and the use of modems (modulator/de-modulator) to convert analog signals to and from digital data. In a packet-switched network, however, the data being exchanged between computers on the network is "encapsulated" within electronic envelopes, also known as packets. Serial communications is generally analogous to a telephone conversation; data is exchanged between two parties in a continuous stream of information, with one party receiving the data in the same order it was sent by the other party. However, the exchange of packets from one computer to another on the network is more similar to mail delivery by the postal service.

Imagine that you write a letter to your Aunt Flo. The letter, when it is completed is several pages long. To deliver the letter, you would normally put it in an envelope, seal the envelope, write Aunt Flo's address on the envelope, include your own return address on the envelope, and remit the envelope into the worthy hands of a postman. But imagine that the government, in its infinite wisdom, passed a law dictating that the Post Office would no longer deliver letters in excess of one page in length. The shrewd writer would quickly recognize an alternate method of delivering a multi-page letter would be to seal each individual page in a separate envelope, address each envelope individually, and mail each envelope as a separate unit. Of course, Aunt Flo might be a little overwhelmed when each page arrived separately and she was forced to re-order the pages in order to read the letter. And imagine the poor postman who would be required to carry an excessively large number of envelopes!

This "single page" Post Office model is similar to packet-switched computing; however, the network computers reassemble the various envelopes automatically once they have arrived at their destination. And instead of the government passing a rather bizarre law requiring each envelope to contain only one page, a telecommunications protocol is used by each computer on the network to regulate packet size; any computer using this protocol agrees to a standard convention which governs the characteristics of the network envelope. Additionally, communications protocols govern the exchange of data identifying the parties sending and receiving data, the identification of the machines which the sender and receiver are using, the number of packets transmitted, and the order in which packets should be arranged upon delivery.

Packet-Switching on Serial Lines

Many users ask, "Why can't packet-switching be performed using my personal computer, a phone line, and my modem?" In fact, this can be done, and we discuss this process in more detail in the section on Serial Line Internet Protocol (SLIP). However, very little packet-switching is currently done over serial lines.

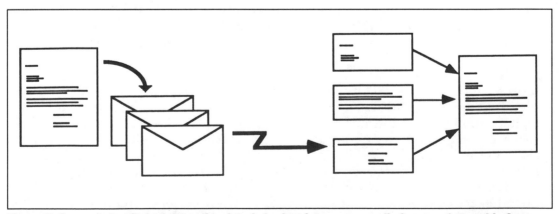

Figure 2. On packet-switched networks, data is broken into many small pieces and stored in framing packets (or electronic envelopes). When the packets are delivered they are opened, the envelopes are discarded, and the original data is reassembled.

Although it is possible to use packet-switching protocols at the slower data rates (300 to 2,400 bits per second) frequently used in asynchronous or synchronous serial data interchange, it is generally not considered viable because of the increased overhead that data encapsulation adds to the transmission process. Consider the following: If you have a 56,000 byte (56 Kbyte) file to transfer on a packet-switched network which uses packets of 56 bytes, the file would be broken into 1,000 pieces. Each of these 1,000 pieces will then be encapsulated into a packet that contains 8 bytes of protocol information telling who sent the packet, where it is headed, and what the packet number is. You now have 1,000 packets each of which are 1,008 bytes in size. The total amount of data to be sent is now 56,448 bytes (56.448 Kbytes).

In a perfect communications channel, at a transmission rate of 1,200 bits per second (one byte equals eight bits), the 56 Kbyte file would take approximately 373 seconds to transmit. However, the larger 56.448 Kbyte file would take 376 seconds to transmit at the same speed. This three-second difference for a 56 Kbyte file does not sound at first like much of a difference. However, when you consider the impact that this overhead would have on data transmission at the mega (million), giga (billion), and tera (trillion) byte levels, it takes on more meaning. Additionally, both error detection/correction in packets and packet disassembly/reassembly have an impact on transmission times. Thus, packet-switching is generally not considered practical at slower data speeds, but is reserved for use in communications channels that have a higher data capacity (also known as "bandwidth").

What Is a Protocol?

The *Hacker's Jargon*, a sometimes sardonic dictionary of hacker terminology which can be searched via the World Wide Web (see Chapter Five: Network Resources), contains the following definitions of protocol, do protocol, and handshaking.

- **protocol**: *n.* As used by hackers, this never refers to the niceties about the proper form for addressing letters to the Papal Nuncio or the order in which one should use the forks in a Russian-style place setting; hackers don't care about such things. It is used instead to describe any set of rules that allow different machines or pieces of software to coordinate with each other without ambiguity. So, for example, it does not include niceties about the proper form for addressing packets on the network or the order in which one should use the forks in the Dining Philosopher Problem. It implies that there is some common message format and an accepted set of primitives or commands that all parties involved understand, and that transactions among them follow predictable logical sequences. See also **handshaking, do protocol.**

- **do protocol**: *[from network protocol programming] vi.* To perform an interaction with somebody or something that follows a clearly defined procedure. For example, "Let's do protocol with the check" at a restaurant means to ask for the check, calculate the tip and everybody's share, collect money from everybody, generate the change necessary, and pay the bill. See also **protocol**.

- **handshaking**: *n.* Hardware or software activity designed to start or keep two machines of programs in synchronization as they do protocol. Often applied to human activity; thus, a hacker might watch two people in conversation nodding their heads to indicate that they have heard each others' points and say "Oh, they're handshaking!" See also **protocol**.

Essentially, protocols are a series of programs, routines, and subroutines, shared by two or more computers. Protocols allow for the unambiguous interchange of data between the computers. In other words, protocols define how disparate machines can inter-operate, and within what boundaries that interaction may take place. Protocols are especially useful in allowing computers with differing operating systems to exchange data over a commonly shared telecommunications channel (a network).

There are a wide variety of protocols available for use on computer networks today. In Chapter One we discussed the reasons for the selection of the Transmission Control Protocol (TCP/IP) suite by the Department of Defense for use on the DARPA Internet, and subsequently for use on the NSFnet. However, there are other protocols routinely used by computers which link to the Internet. Such protocols include, AppleTalk, Token Ring, IPX (Novell NetWare), and X.25. These protocols are sometimes referred to as "feeder" protocols by interested Internet parties because networks based on these protocols serve to feed data into the larger TCP/IP Internet.

Who Writes Protocols?

There are two general methods through which a protocol comes into use. The first method involves the development by a corporation or company of a "proprietary" protocol for use on equipment which it sells. An example of such a protocol is IBM's System Network Architecture (SNA), which was designed specifically for use on IBM equipment. Anyone wishing to use a proprietary protocol must license the use of the protocol from the company owning the rights to it. Of course, the easiest way to do this is generally to buy a company's products, since selling products is almost always the goal of investing in the development of a proprietary protocol.

The second method through which protocol standards come into being is through the activity of formal standards organizations such as the American National Standards Institute (ANSI) and the National Information Standards Organization (NISO). This second channel for protocol publication is often referred to as the "open" standards process, because any corporation (or individual) can participate in the development of standards by becoming a member of the standards organization. Each member can become involved in the development of the standard. Theoretically, the standard that emerges is more robust and has a wider applicability as a result of the larger group participating in the development of the protocol.

Internet Request for Comments (RFCs)

In recent years, Internet development has spawned a third path toward protocol development. This approach involves gathering a group of "hackers" together in a room, and developing protocol specifications concurrently with the applications and inter-operating production systems that will use them. From this process, the Internet Request for Comments (RFC) series was born. Although the RFC series is addressed in more detail in Chapter Five, it is virtually impossible to discuss the development and growth of the Internet and the proposed National Research and Education Network (NREN) without mentioning the RFCs. The RFCs are used by TCP/IP developers to: (1) make available some information for interested people, (2) begin or continue a discussion of an interesting idea, or (3) specify a protocol. It is this third use of RFC which has the most relevance to the topics in this chapter. The RFC is used as the official publication mechanism for the statement of an Internet protocol specification. All developers who choose to implement a service or build an application based on an Internet protocol are expected to follow the standard as it is stated in the corresponding RFC.

Although anyone with an idea for an RFC can prepare a draft-RFC, generally drafts are authored by one of the working groups of the Internet Engineering Task Force (IETF). Because it is helpful to have some application development underway before an RFC is drafted, the working group members often have begun the programming for an application using elements of the draft-RFC.

Once a draft-RFC has been written, it is generally circulated within the network community for comments (thus the name "Request for Comments"). The draft-RFC may be revised as a result of these comments, and is then reviewed by the Internet Engineering Steering Group (IESG). The IESG may also request re-working of the draft-RFC. After being approved by the IESG, and upon the final approval of the Internet Activities Board (IAB), the draft-RFC will become a "draft-Standard." Draft-Standards undergo a similar review process in order to refine them, and upon a second IAB approval a draft-Standard is granted status as a full RFC Standard.

In addition to the RFC process described above, there are two other important maintenance activities related to the TCP/IP protocol suite as it is applied on the Internet. The first is the registration of all of the numerical addresses assigned to hosts on the network (see "Addressing Components" below). This activity is overseen by an agency called the Internet Registry (IR), housed at the Defense Data Network (DDN) Network Information Center:

> Internet Registry
> Defense Data Network Network Information Center
> Government Systems, Inc.
> 14200 Park Meadow Dr., Suite 200
> Chantilly, VA 22021
> (800) 365-3642
> Hostmaster@nic.ddn.mil

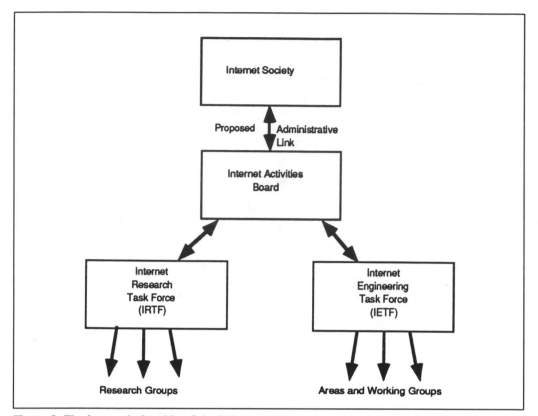

Figure 3. The inter-relationship of the IAB, the IETF, and the Internet Research Task Force.

The second is the assignment of a variety of other registered numbers, such as Internet socket numbers (see "Addressing Components" below), in the TCP/IP Internet. The Internet Assigned Numbers Authority (IANA) oversees this activity.

Internet Assigned Numbers Authority
University of Southern California
Information Sciences Institute
4676 Admiralty Way, Suite 1001
Marina del Rey, CA 90292-6695
iana@isi.edu

The Internetworking Protocols

In Chapters One and Two, we showed that the Internet is actually made up of a myriad of smaller, interconnected networks. All of these networks share a common suite of telecommunication protocols known as the TCP/IP. The Transmission Control Protocol (TCP), the Internet Protocol (IP), and the other protocols that constitute the TCP/IP suite are used by all computers connected to the Internet. Some protocols such as IP are mandatory for any host with a dedicated connection to the network. Other protocols such as the talk, finger, and Post Office Protocol (POP) are optional for hosts on the network, and are needed only by network hosts expected to support specific applications. This close inter-relationship between the Internet and the TCP/IP suite warrants a more a detailed examination of TCP/IP.

The TCP/IP Protocol Suite

As we discussed in Chapter One, TCP/IP owes its current existence as the state-of-the-art in academic/higher education networking to its adoption for use on the DARPA Internet. Through the development of the DARPA Internet, the base TCP/IP suite has been greatly expanded upon, and was subsequently chosen by the National Science Foundation (NSF) as the networking protocol of choice for the emerging National Science Foundation Network (NSFnet). As mentioned above, the development and maintenance of the TCP/IP protocols continue even today through the efforts of the IETF and its working groups.

The TCP/IP is not a single protocol, but is instead a series (often called a "suite") of protocols which interact to control data interchange between hosts on the Internet. TCP/IP is a layered protocol suite not unlike the Open Systems Interconnection (OSI) protocol suite, another commonly used set of networking protocols. In a layered protocol suite, sometimes referred to as a "stack", a series of distinct protocols interact with each other to provide services and applications. Each of these protocols resides within one "layer," and communicates with the protocols in the surrounding (i.e., higher/lower) layers.

Higher Layers	Higher Layers
Transmission Control Protocol (TCP)	User Datagram Protocol (UDP)
Internet Protocol (IP)	
Ethernet	FDDI	Appletalk	Token Ring

Figure 4. From bottom to top: The TCP/IP protocol suite layers are the Network Interconnection layer, the Addressing layer (IP), the Data Transport layer (TCP/UDP), and the Process/Application layer (higher layers).

A closer examination of the TCP/IP protocol suite shows that there are four primary layers: the Network Interconnection (sometimes called Physical) layer, the Addressing (or Network) layer (IP), the Data Transport layer (TCP/UDP), and the Process/Application layer.

The protocols in operation at the Network Interconnection layer, the lowest of the four layers, dictate specifics about the exchange of data with the operating system of the machine and with the physical hardware present on the networked computer. At this layer, TCP/IP communicates with other networking protocols such as AppleTalk, FDDI, or Token Ring.

The second layer of protocol, the Addressing layer, is most often referred to as the Internet Protocol (IP). Each computer on the network has a unique 32-bit address which uniquely identifies it to all other systems on the network. This address allows data intended for the system to be delivered to the proper machine. All other machines on the network will either ignore or forward data packets which do not carry its own unique IP. The IP address is expressed as a series of four 8-bit octets which are separated by periods. Here are three examples of an IP address:

        31.1.1.10   128.100.100.1   192.100.21.1

Because IP addresses are 32-bit numbers, they are expressed as a series of four octets separated by a single period. The numbers fall in the range 1.1.1.1 (1 x 8) through 256.256.256.256 (32 x 8). However, there are certain 32-bit addresses never seen by users of the Internet. These addresses are reserved by the TCP/IP protocol suite for special usage, and cannot be assigned directly to a network computer. One such number is 127.0.0.1, which is reserved by TCP/IP as a "loopback" to the local machine (used for testing purposes). Another example is 255.255.255.255, which is reserved for system use.

The majority of IPs currently in use on the Internet fall into one of three IP classes. These three classes are defined as Class A (first octet falls in the range 1-126), Class B (the first octet falls in the range 128-191), and Class C (first octet falls in the range 192-223). Within an IP, part of the number is used to describe the linking network (campus network, mid-level regional, etc.) and part is used to describe a host computer on that network.

In the table below, *nnn* designates the octet(s) which are used for the network number, and *hhh* designates the octet(s) which are used for the host number. Under this numbering scheme, there are 128 Class A networks, 16,384 Class B networks, and 2,097,152 Class C networks possible. Class D and Class E networks exist, but cannot currently be used for host applications. Although there are fewer Class A networks, a Class A network can have more hosts within it. Conversely, there can be fewer hosts on each class C network, although there are many more Class C network assignments.

Class	First Octet	IP address	Number of nets
Class	A?1-126	nnn.hhh.hhh.hhh	128
Class B	128-191	nnn.nnn.hhh.hhh	16,384
Class C	192-223	nnn.nnn.nnn.hhh	2,097,152

The third layer of the TCP/IP protocol suite is the Data Transport layer. Two protocols are generally used at this layer in the protocol suite: the TCP and the User Datagram Protocol (UDP). It is highly likely that a system on the Internet will support both of these protocols. This can be attributed to the fact that there are many different Process/Application layer protocols in use which require one or the other of these Data Transport protocols. Therefore, in order to have a wider selection of Process/Application protocol choices, most implementations of TCP/IP stacks support both TCP and UDP. However, each higher level application will use only TCP or UDP, not both. The Data Transport protocol(s) controls information such as the size of packets, the number of packets that comprise an entire transmission, and the format of the data in the packet.

The final layer of the TCP/IP protocol suite is the Process or Application protocol layer. These protocols are most likely to be of interest to the reader, as this layer governs the operation of the actual end-user applications used to communicate between hosts on the network. There are many application protocols in existence on the network—indeed, more than can be considered in a work of this scope. In the following pages, however, we will review several of the most significant application layer protocols, including Telnet, the File Transmission Protocol (FTP), and the Simple Mail Transfer Protocol (SMTP). Some protocols that are less widely implemented in the Internet such as the finger protocol and the POP will be discussed briefly. Finally, the potential of some protocols that are not unique to the TCP/IP Internet, but are being implemented in the TCP/IP Internet, will be considered.

At this point, it is important to understand that not all of the applications described here are available on every system in the Internet. Although it is unlikely that you will find a host on the Internet which does not support Telnet, and most hosts support an implementation of FTP, other applications may not necessarily be available on a given host. Which applications are available to a computing user ultimately depends on many factors such as:

- The operating system being used on the Internet host; not all applications have been ported to (implemented for) every operating system.
- Decisions of the system administrator; it may not be feasible to consume computing resources to support certain protocols on a given system.
- Similarly, some system administrators will decide not to support a certain protocol in favor of supporting another since the services provided by a few protocols are quite similar.
- The cost of licensing such an application; although the protocols that govern the development of applications in TCP/IP lie within the public domain (i.e., they are open protocols), some specific implementations of applications based on those protocols are commercial or proprietary.

The "Big Three" TCP/IP Application Protocols

Specific numbers are difficult to extract from statistics on network traffic. Nevertheless, there can be little doubt that Telnet, FTP, and SMTP usage constitutes an extremely significant portion of the entire traffic that traverses the Internet daily. For this reason, these applications have been referred to as the "big three" TCP/IP applications. Of these three, SMTP, which handles the transmission of electronic mail, probably accounts for the greatest portion of network traffic.

With a firm understanding of the promise more sophisticated networked applications offer, one can easily see that the existing implementations of process/ application layer protocols which are most commonly used on the Internet today are, in a word, barbaric. Indeed, the "big three" applications pale by comparison to some of the more sophisticated client/server applications currently under development. We will explore these applications in more detail in Chapter Four.

To the network neophyte, one who has had little or no contact with the Internet, it may be difficult to explain why these applications should be considered barbaric. Nevertheless, using the DARPA Internet frame of reference, one should recognize that these three applications are quite aged. All three of these protocols are widely implemented for use on time-share hosts which support character-based terminals, and this undoubtedly accounts to a large extent for their immense popularity. The 80 x 24 character-based terminal emulation mode currently provides the lowest common denominator in computing applications on the network.

But consider that much has happened in the development of computing systems in the past twenty years. The microchip brought computing into the home and to the desktops of people everywhere. Fiber optics have allowed for the transmission of data at speeds which were inconceivable two decades ago. And developments in both disk storage and random access memory have made it possible to put computing power previously reserved for the elite few with access to super-expensive, super-powerful, supercomputers on the desktop of the graduate students in dormitory rooms. By these standards, terminal emulation applications, such as the vast majority of existing Telnet, FTP, and SMTP implementations, must be recognized as the highly reliable, although largely unglamorous, network workhorses that they are.

Telnet

Telnet, as specified in RFC854, is an application protocol which is used to allow a host on the Internet to emulate a terminal circuit with any other host on the Internet. Most Telnet applications emulate an ANSI line mode terminal and/or a VT100 terminal. When Telnet is executed, the local host on the network becomes a "virtual terminal" to the remote host elsewhere on the network. Using this application, a user can login to a remote host on the network, and run software which resides on that host and read data files residing on that host. Most implementations of Telnet expect the user to have a valid login ID and password on the remote host (see below). Yet, some specific implementations of Telnet applications allow the user to use a generally distributed login ID and password for read-only access to the system.

There are many different implementations of the Telnet protocol, and the usage among these implementations varies somewhat. However, the most common line mode emulation implementations of Telnet, generally uses this syntax:

```
<path> Telnet <address> <port>
```

where:

> <path> is a directive path statement which allows the operating system to locate an executable image or file.

> Telnet is the name of the executable image.

> <address> is either the IP or the canonical name of the target host in the Internet.

> <port> is the Internet socket number to be used (explained under "Addressing Components"). This argument can generally be omitted from the command, and the Telnet default socket number of 23 will be used.

tn3270

The tn3270 application is an implementation of the Telnet protocol which allows for the emulation of the IBM native terminal type, tn3270. Implementations of tn3270 are fairly common for Macintosh computers, UNIX workstations, and VAX minicomputers where the native terminal type is generally a VT100. Without tn3270 terminal control these computers and other computers using a native terminal type of VT100 are generally unable to communicate with systems requiring full-screen tn3270 terminal emulation. Remote hosts which most commonly require full-screen tn3270 emulation are IBM mainframes operating the VM and/or MVS operating systems, and most often running VM/CMS full-screen emulation applications. On a line mode terminal, the syntax for tn3270 is generally similar to that of Telnet:

> <path> tn3270 <address> <port>

where:

> <path> is a directive path statement which allows the operating system to locate an executable image or file.

> tn3270 is the name of the executable image.

> <address> is either the IP or the canonical name of the target host in the Internet.

> <port> is the Internet socket number to be used (explained under "Addressing Components"). This argument can generally be omitted from the command, and the Telnet default socket number of 23 will be used.

File Transmission Protocol (FTP)

The second of the "big three" application layer protocols is the File Transmission Protocol (FTP). FTP is specified in RFC959, and is used to move files between hosts on the Internet. It is possible to move a file from the local host to a remote host (upload), or move a file from a remote host to a local host (download), using FTP. To the reader who may have encountered electronic bulletin board systems (bbs), this type of activity is nothing new. The main difference between FTP and dial-up bulletin board systems is the rate of transfer between hosts on the network. Using FTP, it is possible to transfer files which are hundreds of thousands of bytes in size between hosts on the network in a matter of seconds. The experienced computer bbs user will know that downloading a file of similar size at a rate of 1,200bps, if one were daring enough to undertake such a task, could possibly take a significant portion of an hour!

The FTP protocol accommodates the transfer of multiple file formats. Most FTP applications in use on the network provide for the transfer of textual files (in both ASCII and EBCDIC modes) and also for the transfer of binary image files. For more information on these formats, see "File Formats in the Internet," below.

Another feature of the FTP application is its support for anonymous file transfer and storage—or "anonymous FTP." Anonymous FTP allows system administrators the ability to mount files on network hosts for public consumption without administering login IDs and passwords. Similarly, network users can use anonymous FTP as a method for accessing these public files without having to apply with a system administrator for a login ID and password on the remote host. For more detailed information on anonymous FTP, see Chapter Four.

Again, specific implementations of the FTP protocol vary greatly. However, on a line mode terminal the syntax for the FTP protocol is generally:

        <path> FTP <address> <port>

where:

> <path> is a directive path statement which allows the operating system to locate an executable image or file.
>
> FTP is the name of the FTP program.
>
> <address> is either the IP or the canonical name of the target host in the Internet.
>
> <port> is the Internet socket number to be used (explained under "Addressing Components"). This argument can generally be omitted from the command, and the Telnet default socket number of 23 will be used.

Simple Mail Transfer Protocol (SMTP)

Every day, hundreds of thousands, perhaps even millions, of electronic mail notes are transmitted on the Internet, and through Internet gateways to global networks beyond. The Simple Mail Transfer Protocol (SMTP) is used to govern the exchange of those electronic mail notes between the various hosts on the Internet, and to negotiate the transfer of electronic mail through the Internet gateways.

SMTP is a network standard which is fully described in the RFC821. As mentioned, existing implementations of network applications are relatively underdeveloped at this juncture. However, unlike Telnet and FTP, the user is largely shielded from the language of the SMTP protocol transactions because the interface to SMTP applications is more sophisticated in the vast majority of cases. These protocol transactions are generally conducted automatically by SMTP "mailing agents" which reside on the network hosts, although it is possible to force such transactions to be conducted manually on some systems, generally for debugging purposes. On a few occasions, an electronic mail note may be returned to a user as "undeliverable." In those instances, the mailing agent will generally return a portion of the SMTP transaction log to the person who sent the note to assist the person in determining what went wrong. Some familiarity with an SMTP transaction can assist the user at that point.

One can generally determine if a host on the Internet supports the SMTP protocol by executing a Telnet session against port 25 of the target address:

```
<path> Telnet <address> 25
```

where:

<path> is a directive path statement which allows the operating system to locate an executable image or file.

Telnet is the name of the Telnet executable program.

<address> is either the IP or the canonical name of the target host in the Internet.

25 is the Internet socket number (explained under "Addressing Components") to be used. This is the default port number for SMTP transactions.

If the host at the target address supports SMTP, you should receive a message similar to this:

```
220 <host.domain> Sendmail 5.57/net_11/01/91 ready at
Sun, 24 May 92
QUIT
```

Addressing Components

Addressing is a term used to designate a user and/or machine's location on the network. There are three components of network addressing which the user should fully understand. The need to understand these three components will arise frequently when the user begins to use TCP/IP applications. These three addressing components are the login ID used to distinguish another person on an Internet host, the address of a host on the network, and thirdly, in a few instances, the address of a gateway router which is used as a data transfer path between two hosts on the network. This third component is most often not needed in Internet addressing, but there are times when understanding gateway routers can be useful.

User Login ID

Current estimates indicate that there are approximately 727,000 computers on the Internet [RFC1296]. Certainly, a great number of those computers are time-share systems which allow more than one user to access the system at the same time. IBM mainframes, DEC VAX minicomputers, and the recently introduced workstations based on RISC processor technology are all examples of systems that are capable of supporting multiple simultaneous usage. On the other hand, PCs and Macintosh computers generally support only a single user at one time.

On time-share systems, it is necessary for each user to have a unique code which will identify them during the sign-on (or logon) process. This unique code can be used by the operating system to prevent unauthorized access to the user's data files and to control access to sensitive executable code on the system. In this text, we refer to these unique login codes as a user's login ID.

The nature of login IDs varies widely from system to system on the Internet. Some login IDs are relatively easy to remember. For example, Craig Summerhill uses the login ID "craig" on the Coalition for Networked Information's DEC 5000/200 file server. Other login IDs are less intuitive. It is not at all uncommon to find a login ID which is some seemingly arbitrary string of letters and numbers, such as "abcd123."

Several factors govern how a user's login ID is constructed. Certain operating systems place limitations on the construction of login IDs. For example, the VM operating system for IBM mainframes will not support login IDs of more than eight characters. For persons whose name exceeds eight characters, this can present a problem. One of this book's authors has had the login ID of SUMMERHI on VM/CMS mainframes on more than one occasion for that reason. Another factor governing the construction of login IDs includes the system manager's personal method of managing such login IDs. Since each login ID must be unique, persons by the name John Smith and Jane Smith could not be assigned the same login ID of SMITH. There are many options which a system manager can take to assign unique login IDs to each of these persons. Some possible solutions to the need for a unique login ID for each of these users are:

John D. Smith	Jane A. Smith
SMITH1	SMITH2
JOHN_SMITH	JANE_SMITH
JDSMITH	JASMITH

When another person gives you his/her login ID, you should remember that it may appear much more random than it actually is. Looking for a hidden pattern can actually assist in remembering a person's login ID. Of course, on systems with a need for greater security, one method employed in the assignment of login IDs is to use a program that randomly generates a string of letters and/or numbers to create a login ID. Trying to discern a pattern in those types of login IDs might be frustrating.

Machine Address (Node Name)

Just as each user on a time-share machine must have a unique designation, each machine on the network must also have a unique network designation. This designation is referred to as a machine's address. Sometimes a machine's address is referred to as its "node" on the network. There are two methods used in the Internet to express the unique address of a machine: numerical addressing and canonical name addressing.

<u>Numerical Addressing (IP)</u>

Each host system registered on the Internet is assigned a unique numerical address. This numerical address is expressed as a 32-bit number, and it is referred to as an Internet Protocol (IP) address. An IP address is divided into four 8-bit octets, and is generally expressed as a number in the form such as:

    nnn.hhh.hhh.hhh

where:

> nnn is the first octet which is used to describe a network, in this case a Class A network. Each of the other three 8-bit octets (hhh) are separated from the net octet by single periods, and represent the host address.

As noted above, IPs are assigned by the Internet Registry.

<u>Canonical Name Addressing</u>

Unfortunately, numerical addresses assigned to machines on the network are sometimes difficult to remember. Imagine trying to remember the telephone numbers of all the people responsible for all 727,000+ computers currently on the Internet. Undoubtedly an impossible task! Remembering an IP address for every one of these hosts is equally impossible. For this reason, an alternate method of machine addressing has been developed for use on the Internet. In this addressing scheme, each machine is assigned a unique "canonical name." The canonical name is a mnemonic address designed to aid recall, enhance accessibility to the machine by users on the network, and provide for enhanced security measures on machines containing sensitive data.

A distributed naming scheme automatically translates from canonical name to IP address, and allows the design of tools to facilitate the location of resources on the network. This name resolution scheme is often referred to as "host/domain resolution" or "name resolution." One of the most common applications in use on the network for host/domain resolution is the Berkeley Internet Name Domain service (BIND). Machines running BIND actually participate in the management of a very large distributed database. Any single BIND server stores both the numerical address and the canonical name address of the machines registered within its region in the local tables, and other remote BIND servers can contact it for information on the machines in the local region as needed.

Numerical address	Canonical name
35.1.1.42	merit.edu
192.112.36.5	nic.ddn.mil
192.80.214.100	noc.sura.net

Hosts and Domains

The canonical address designation often contains specific information about the geographic location of a machine, and the organization owning and operating the machine. This information about various regions of the Internet is concealed in a structured domain naming scheme. A person who understands how to decipher a computer's canonical address can use it to learn a considerable amount of information about the computer and the organization maintaining it.

Consider the following canonical names:

WSUVM1.csc.wsu.edu
noc.sura.net
library.andrew.cmu.edu
bobcat.csc.wsu.edu

The first thing that is readily apparent about these addresses is that three of them share a similar designation in the final 8-bit suffix of the address, which is used to indicate the "top-level domain." Top-level domains are the broadest classification in the naming schema, and group together organizations of similar type without regard to the individual computer system.

The suffix .EDU indicates that this computer is run by an educational institution in the United States. Other current top-level domains include (but are not limited to):

.gov	United States Federal Government agencies
.mil	United States Military Installations
.com	Commercial Organizations (i.e., Businesses)
.org	Not-for-Profit Organizations
.ca	Canada
.jp	Japan
.us	United States

The .EDU, .GOV, .MIL, .COM, and .ORG domains designate specific types of top-level networks which are for the most part made up of machines located within the United States. In addition, a number of countries now have their own top-level domains.

A careful look at the canonical names, shown above, reveals another pattern. The addresses bobcat.csc.wsu.edu and WSUVM1.csc.wsu.edu both are similar. The experienced networker will recognize that the domain WSU.EDU is part of the canonical name assigned to all machines owned by Washington State University (WSU). The .CSC portion of the name indicates that the machines are located within the Computing Service Center at WSU. Finally, the individual computers are named WSUVM1 and BOBCAT. (In "real-life," WSUVM1 is an IBM 3090 running VM/CMS and MVS, and BOBCAT is a VAX 11/785 that is part of the Computing Service Center's VAX cluster.)

Although the process of deciphering canonical names may seem daunting, in fact, there are a number of consistent features of these names that make them easier for users to identify. In the example above, the host name WSUVM1, the operating system VM appears in the name; thus, it is likely an IBM mainframe of some kind.

The judicious use of other network tools such as Telnet, FTP, and finger (see below) will yield additional clues to the network traveler.

The other canonical names listed above can be deciphered as:

noc.sura.net	The Network Operations Center at SURAnet (within the sura.net domain)
library.andrew.cmu.edu	The LIS II Library System at Carnegie Mellon University (within the cmu.edu domain)

Internet Ports/Sockets

Internet ports (also known as Internet sockets) are used as an extension to machine addressing. In addition to a numerical IP address or host/domain address, almost every application on the network requires the use of an Internet socket. Many application layer protocols are designed to use a specific socket, which is included as a default during execution of a program such as Telnet or FTP. For this reason, many users of the network never realize that an Internet socket is being used, much less that it is required.

Each network application must use its own unique and reserved socket number. For this reason, the assignment of Internet sockets (port numbers) are regulated by the Internet Assigned Numbers Authority (IANA). However, before an official socket number is issued to a software developer, a short survey must be filled out and submitted to IANA. Upon the receipt and processing of the survey, the IANA will assign a unique socket number for use with a specific application. From that point forward, that designated socket number is reserved on all standard implementations of TCP/IP for use by the designated protocol/application for which it has been assigned.

UNIX systems running TCP/IP have a file detailing the protocols being supported on the machine, and the corresponding socket assignment. On most UNIX systems this is the /etc/services file. This file is generally a good sampling of Internet socket number assignments. Below is a selection of socket assignments from an /etc/services file. Remember, these socket numbers will be the same on all hosts on the network which support the Process/Application protocol in question. Some of the protocols shown in this table are reviewed later in this chapter.

Login IDs, the IP, and Host/Domain Addresses

The individual elements of network addressing that a user must specify depends on the type of application being used. As a general rule, applications that are "connection-oriented" (i.e., real-time connections between two computers on the network) require a machine address to be stated by the user. Telnet and FTP are such applications. When executing a connection-oriented application, a socket number must be designated, although this designation sometimes occurs by default. In this example, the user is establishing a connection to the host foo.bar.com using the Internet port 2225.

```
Telnet foo.bar.com 2225
```

In addition to a machine address and Internet socket, other applications, such as the delivery of electronic mail using the SMTP, will require the user to provide a login ID. The syntax for beginning an interactive session with a mailing agent on most systems in the Internet is something like:

```
mail <loginID>@<host.domain>
```

For example:

```
mail craig@cni.org
mail dave@foo.bar.com
```

The @ symbol is used to designate the separation of the login ID and machine address elements by most Internet mailing agents. On other networks, and even in some implementations of mailers for machines within the Internet, this delimiting character may be different. For example, some IBM VM/CMS mailers accept the word "at" instead of "or" in addition to the @ symbol:

```
mail craig at cni.org
```

Mail transfer over the Internet using UNIX to UNIX CoPy protocol (UUCP) often requires the syntax shown below. Fortunately, this type of syntax is becoming less common among Internet hosts as point-to-point SMTP transactions continue to become more predominant:

```
mail cni-gw!a!craig
```

If an address using the @ sign does not work, check with your local system administrator for the appropriate syntax. On occasion, the user may find that she/he needs to know the address of a gateway router, described in the next section.

Using Gateway Addressing

The first two components of network addressing, discussed above, were the user login ID and the machine address (either numerical IP or canonical name). The third, and final, component of network addressing—which is less frequently used by persons on the network—is the gateway address. The gateway address is used to establish a connection between the user's local host or network and the remote host or network.

At one stage in network evolution, the need for knowledge of gateways was much more important than it is now. Advances in the development of the name/domain resolution scheme, an increasingly improved network topology, and the advent of more experienced system administrators who are capable of building "seamless" network links to other networks in the Internet, are rapidly eliminating the need for users to interact explicitly with gateways. Nevertheless, it is almost inevitable that you will have a "close encounter" with a network gateway eventually, if you use electronic mail with any frequency.

From the casual user's perspective, gateway addressing is used almost exclusively for sending electronic mail from the Internet to a user whose login ID and host address are on a network only peripherally linked to the Internet. Of course, most gateways can also be used to send electronic mail from the remote network to users on the Internet also.

The use of a network gateway inevitably adds to the complexity of addressing. However, the actual form and amount of this added complexity varies greatly among gateways on the network. Some network gateways are relatively simple to use. For example, users on the Internet can routinely route data to one of several BITNET gateways.

A user on BITNET would send mail to another BITNET node using the following addressing convention:

LOGINID@NODENAME

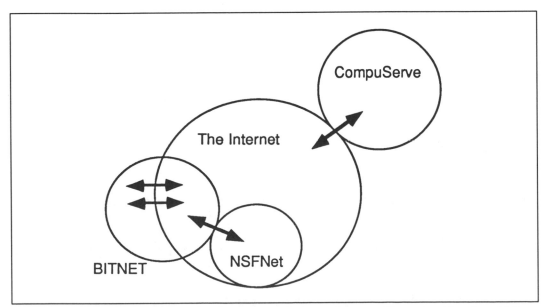

Figure 5. Gateways (sometimes called bridges) are linkages between disparate networks which are used to pass data between the hosts on those differing networks. In this diagram, the arrows indicate the potential location of some bridges on the networks shown.

And a user on the Internet would use the following addressing convention to reach a node on the BITNET:

```
loginid@nodename.bitnet
```

A BITNET user, whose login ID is located on a machine without a direct Internet connection, might reach an Internet host using the following addressing convention. CUNYVM is the name of a BITNET host which has an Internet gateway attached:

```
LOGINID%host.domain@CUNYVM
```

Similarly, Internet users can send mail to users of the CompuServe commercial information service by using a relatively easy gateway addressing syntax. (The procedure for sending mail between CompuServe and the Internet is described in Chapter Two.)

The final example of gateway addressing convention demonstrates the potential complexity of gateway addressing. Merit Computing, Inc. operates a gateway between the Internet and the SprintMail network. SprintMail can inter-operate with the Internet via SprintNet (formally Telenet). Because SprintMail/SprintNet uses a mail protocol known as X.400 rather than SMTP, addressing conventions for data transfers between the two networks are substantially more complicated for the user.

A user on the Internet can send mail to a SprintMail customer using this addressing convention:

```
/C=US/ADMD=TELEMAIL/O=ORGANIZATION/G=GIVENNAME/S=SURNAME/
@SPRINT.COM
```

A SprintMail customer can reach the Internet using this addressing convention:

```
loginid@host.domain:
(C=USA,A:Telemail,P:Internet,"RFC822".<loginid
(a)host.domain>)
```

Selecting a Mailer

There are dozens of mailing agents that can be used on Internet hosts. In fact, it is not uncommon for larger Internet hosts, such as IBM mainframes or VAX minicomputers, to have more than one mailing agent available to users. To a great degree, the choice of a mail system is a matter of personal preference. Just as some people prefer chocolate ice cream to vanilla ice cream, some people will prefer to use the Extended Berkeley Mailer rather than the ELM mailer (both are well-known mailers for hosts running the UNIX operating system).

Chances are, as a network neophyte, you will not be immediately faced with major decisions regarding the purchase and implementation of a mail system. In most cases, you will be presented with one mailer for your electronic mail needs, and your only decision will be whether or not to use it. In some cases, your system may have more than one mailer available. If this is the case, there will probably be a system administrator within your organization who can assist you in determining which mail system will best meet your needs. If there are several mail systems readily available, experiment with each of them by sending mail to yourself. Find out for yourself which one best suits your style of reading and sending of mail.

In the unlikely event that you are in the position of making a decision about the installation of a mail system for an Internet host, be sure to acquire a mail system that is compliant with the Internet RFCs pertaining to the transmission of electronic mail. If you expect to exchange mail with other hosts on the Internet, the mailer must support the SMTP standard as stated in the most current release of RFC821. Compliance with "The Standard for the format of ARPA Internet Text Messages," as outlined in RFC822, is also recommended. If you are not sure whether the mailer that you are considering is compliant with these RFCs, check around with other experienced networking people. Contact the campus computing center or the network operations center of a mid-level network near you (see the list of mid-level regionals in Chapter Two). If you have access to Usenet newsgroups, ask questions on comp.mail.misc. Find a person who has been on the network for a while! Consulting with an expert user can result in a recommendation that saves you a lot of time, and possibly some money.

Additional Readings on Network Addressing
It is not our intention to demonstrate all possible network addressing formulas in this book. Such a comprehensive accounting of network addressing would be nearly impossible. However, there are several sources which we recommend for further reading on the topic of electronic mail gateways and addressing conventions:

Frey, D., & Adams, R. (1990). *!%@: A directory of electronic mail addressing and networks*. (Sebastopol, CA: O'Reilly and Associates).

La Quey, T. L. (1990). *The user's directory of computer networks*. (Bedford, MA: Digital Press).

Quarterman, J. S. (1990). *The matrix: computer networks and conferencing systems worldwide*. (Bedford, MA: Digital Press).

Other Common Internet Protocols

Some other protocols that are specified for implementation in the TCP/IP Internet, or are commonly associated with the network by its users, are described below. This list is by no means complete. Readers interested in a more complete overview of the "standard" protocol implementations in the Internet should consult to RFC1250, "IAB Official Protocol Standards" by Jon Postel, and the related RFCs cited therein.

Finger Protocol
RFC1288 defines a protocol for the exchange of user information between hosts in the Internet. The finger protocol, as outlined in RFC1288 and the earlier RFC742,

was originally programmed by Les Earnest at the Stanford Artificial Intelligence Laboratory (SAIL). Most implementations of the finger protocol are for the BSD (Berkeley Systems) UNIX operating system; however, the finger protocol is supported by many VAX/VMS computers also.

Information on the use of Finger applications is provided in Chapter Four.

Network News Transfer Protocol (NNTP)

The Network News Transfer Protocol (NNTP) specifies the distribution, inquiry, retrieval, and posting of news articles between Internet hosts. For the purposes of the NNTP protocol, "news" is defined as bulletins and information about a wide range of topics. The best-known implementation of network news is the Usenet network, a distributed conferencing system. On the Usenet network, each host has a connection to one or more other hosts. News is distributed between those hosts via a process of large-scale downloads, in which one host on the network copies the news "article" to every other host to which it is connected. Such a chain-link connection is referred to as a "news feed." Unfortunately, these news feeds generally require massive amounts of disk storage in order to accommodate the large quantities of data downloaded. (The Usenet news network is described in more detail in Chapters Two and Four.)

The electronic "mailing list" method of distributing information (also described in Chapter Four), in contrast, is exceptionally wasteful of network bandwidth because multiple copies of each message are delivered across the network.

NNTP allows news articles to be stored in a central database, as they are in Usenet. However, unlike Usenet, NNTP uses conventional connection-oriented links (real-time connections) between the reader's local host and the host housing the central database elsewhere on the network. The user can subscribe to only those topics in which she/he has an interest. Indexing, cross-referencing, and expiration of aged messages are also specified. NNTP is detailed more fully in RFC977.

Post Office Protocol (POP)

The Post Office Protocol (POP), as described in RFC1225 and RFC1082, outlines a transaction process for the exchange of electronic mail between two computers. Under POP, one network computer acts as a server host and the other acts as a client host. The protocol is designed to allow clients on the network to dynamically retrieve electronic mail from a mailbox server. The mailbox server would generally be a large time-sharing computer (such as a mainframe, minicomputer, or RISC workstation), while the client would be a desktop workstation (such as a PC, Mac, or workstation). The mailbox server would store a user's electronic mail indefinitely, until that user's POP client software contacted the mailbox. Upon this contact, the mailbox server would forward all waiting mail to the client host.

There are several advantages to using a POP client for electronic mail. Although it can be quite convenient to receive mail on a personal computer, it is not always realistic to expect a desktop computer to be constantly powered on, A standard SMTP mail server, however, is generally expected to be running twenty-four hours a day to receive mail (one can never tell when a message will arrive; a message sent from Finland will most likely arrive in the wee hours of the morning in the United States).

Additionally, the use of a POP client can provide an e-mail user with an interface with which she/he is familiar. A Macintosh user can use a Macintosh client, while a PC user can use a DOS or Windows client. A person using a POP client does not need to become intimately familiar with the mail system used on the mailbox server (a system more often than not selected by a system administrator who has little knowledge of the computing skills and needs of the end-user).

A user may be able to initiate a POP session from anywhere on the network. For example, undergraduate students could theoretically use any machine in one of several microcomputer labs on the campus to check their mail, by carrying a disk with them that contains the POP client. If the same disk also is used to store the downloaded mail, the POP client can be used to read those files at any time of the day or night—even when used on a machine that is not connected to the network. Replies to mail can be stored on the disk until the next time a network connection is available. At that time they are uploaded to the network and delivered to the intended recipient via the POP server. Therefore, another advantage of POP clients is that they can help reduce the active connection time required to use a mail system.

The final advantage of using a POP mail system is that POP can greatly reduce the amount of disk storage space required on the larger host system for storage and processing of e-mail. When notes are downloaded from the server to the client, it frees disk space that would otherwise be used to store those notes. Of course, from the user's perspective, this may not always be an advantage, because it places an even greater burden of disk space management on the user. If notes are not properly archived or erased, a user will quickly overflow a disk or PC hard disk which is being used to store incoming mail. However, for many users the advantages of the POP client/server mail will be worthwhile.

Simple Network Management Protocol (SNMP)

The casual network user will probably never come into contact with SNMP, the core of which is outlined in RFC1157. However, this protocol is endorsed by the Internet Activities Board (IAB) as the short-intermediate range network management protocol, and for this reason system administrators in the Internet are likely to be intimately familiar with it. Even those persons who are responsible for the administration of small TCP/IP zones or sub-nets may have cause to use the protocol. SNMP has been defined for use over IPX (such as Novell NetWare) and also over the Open System Interconnection (OSI).

Related Protocols

Other protocols being designed and implemented for use in the TCP/IP Internet, or commonly associated with the network by its users, are described below. As in the section above, this list is by no means complete. The origins and publication of these protocols are widely varied.

Hypertext Text Transfer Protocol (HTTP)

The HTTP is a Process/Application layer protocol, compatible with TCP/IP, that lies within the public domain. HTTP uses TCP to deliver textual information over the Internet. Connections to HTTP systems generally use a Telnet connection to an Internet host which operates an HTTP system at a specific socket/port number.

HTTP is used to design information systems containing Hypertext links. The server will generally display a top-level menu to users upon connection. Below this top-level menu is a series of subordinate menus or screens that can contain textual information on a wide variety of topics. Hyper links between these screens allow the user to move in a non-linear fashion throughout the information system in a manner similar to that employed by personal computer-based programs like Apple's HyperCard and IBM's Toolbook.

Although it does not completely comply with standard HTTP, the best-known current implementation of an HTTP-like system is the World Wide Web (W3), a system operated at the European Particle Physics Laboratory in Geneva, Switzerland (see Chapter Five).

Internet Gopher

The Internet Gopher protocol is a TCP/IP Process/Application protocol, specifying a client/server methodology for the searching and retrieval of textual data over the Internet. The Internet Gopher protocol, and the best-known clients and servers by the same name, were developed at the University of Minnesota. The University encourages use of and experimentation with the protocol.

Delivery of textual information between clients and servers in the Internet is the goal of the Gopher protocol. Resources, including those located on different servers widely dispersed on the network, are presented to the user as a series of menu screens similar to that of the HTTP-based World Wide Web. However, the Gopher protocol presents the information as a highly structured hierarchy, as opposed to the seemingly structureless presentation offered by HTTP. The hierarchical approach taken by Gopher—a main menu and a virtually infinite number of submenus—is ideal for introducing new users to the world of network resources. Advanced network users, who know precisely what they wish to locate, are likely to find the relative inflexibility of the Gopher system frustrating.

Detailed information on the protocol can be obtained from the Gopher development team via e-mail using the Internet address gopher@boombox.micro.umn.edu. More information on the Gopher application can also be found in Chapter Four.

Kermit

Kermit was not originally a TCP/IP-based protocol, although it has been adapted for use on Ethernet networks. Developed at Columbia University in the early 1980s, Kermit is actually an error-correcting file transfer protocol with several distinct layers of its own, and was originally designed for use on dial-up serial connections. Kermit supports the transfer of both binary and textual file formats. Although Kermit is not generally used for communication between TCP/IP hosts on the Internet, it is quite commonly used for file transfer between Internet hosts and personal computers connected to them via serial lines (computers with Phase Two connectivity, as described earlier in this chapter).

Open Systems Interconnection (OSI)

The Open Systems Interconnection (OSI) is a well-developed layered protocol suite which is primarily the product of several European standards organizations (the foremost of which is the International Organisation for Standardisation [ISO]). A full OSI "stack" includes seven layers of operation. For this reason it has been criticized by some network experts as being too unwieldy for implementation on existing networks. Critics charge that implementations which follow the standard to the letter require unnecessary amounts of processing, and point to the TCP/IP Internet as an example of a more simplified protocol stack. On the other hand, OSI has fully developed protocol specifications for certain features such as security/access control and resource auditing/accounting which would have to be built as application layer protocols in a TCP/IP stack (but are more generally ignored in the TCP/IP Internet).

Most often, when people say that they use an OSI network, they actually are using the X.25 interface between data terminal equipment (DTE) and data-circuit terminating equipment (DCE). Full OSI implementations do not currently exist for the reasons stated above, and because of a lack of commercially available hard-

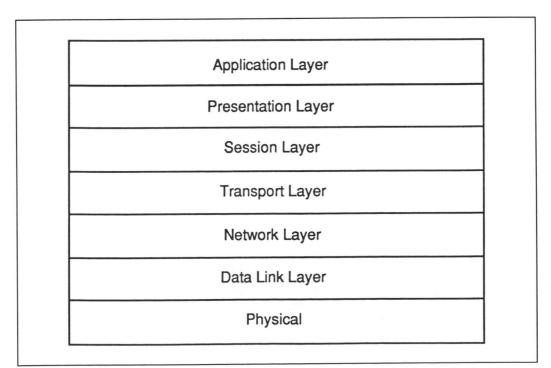

Figure 6. The Open Systems Interconnection model is similar to TCP/IP. However it incorporates two layers (Presentation and Session) which are not included in the TCP/IP specifications. Additionally, TCP/IP treats the Physical and Data Link layers as a single layer.

ware to support the OSI specifications. A diagram of the seven layers of the OSI protocol suite is shown below.

Following the receipt in 1987 by Merit Computing, Inc of an NSF grant to re-engineer the NSFnet, there was much speculation about the relationship between OSI and TCP/IP. Considerable discussion ensued over the idea of the largest circuits of the TCP/IP Internet (i.e., those at the national level) migrating from the TCP/IP protocols to the OSI protocols as the network grew. This migration would take place over the course of a decade, perhaps two.

Such speculation remains today. However, faced with the astronomical network growth of the late 1980s and early 1990s, an increasingly larger portion of the network service community is talking about building gigabit (billions of bits per second) and terabit (trillions of bits per second) level networks, based upon entirely different protocol suites. In some cases, these protocol suites are purely theoretical; they are based purely on paper, with no arena for practical implementation yet available. Thus, the relationship of the OSI protocols to the emerging global Internet is uncertain, although it seems evident that OSI implementations will continue to be developed to link into the global Internet via gateways.

This scenario, of OSI feeder networks linking to a much larger global infrastructure, is troubling for many in the community of library technologists, due to the large investment the library world has placed in OSI technology. Companies such as OCLC and RLIN have existing X.25 infrastructures, and strategic plans for continued development of OSI networks. A detailed examination of the differences between the pro-OSI and pro-TCP/IP contingents is beyond the scope of this work. A thoughtful consideration of the relationship of OSI to TCP/IP is already included in Lorcan Dempsey's *Libraries, Networks, and OSI* [1991]. Interested readers should refer to that work for more detailed information.

Prospero

Prospero is a protocol, and an application of the protocol, which is designed to organize data over wide area networks. Designed and implemented by Clifford Neuman of the University of Washington, Prospero is built around a virtual system model of data organization. In this virtual system, the user is not required to download files to local hosts for storage. When a user finds a document of interest on the network, she/he makes a note of it using the Prospero system. From that point forward, Prospero tracks the object (directory, file, binary) in the wide area network and updates reference pointers on a user's local machine each time an action (delete, move, update) is taken on the object at the remote host on the network. Theoretically, a user only needs to consult the Prospero system to determine the exact location of any object if it is needed again in the future. The Prospero protocol is still largely experimental. The INFO-PROSPERO@CS.WASHINGTON.EDU mailing list is being used to distribute information about the protocol as it develops to interested parties.

Serial Line Internet Protocol (SLIP)

SLIP is not actually a Process/Application layer protocol, but is a Networking layer protocol similar to IP. Currently, there is no Internet standard governing the encapsulation of IP packets which are to be transmitted over serial lines. However, the SLIP packet-framing protocol is being widely implemented, and may be becoming a de facto standard for serial line IP encapsulation. It has gained popularity among mid-level service providers and campus computing centers because it can be adapted to dynamically assign an IP address to a machine for the time it is connected to the network via a dial-up line. The dynamic assignment of IP addresses allows a group of users to share a smaller number of IP addresses, while still providing them with the advantages of Phase Three connectivity. However, this process is an extension to the SLIP protocol. The negotiation of these host IP addresses is not directly specified by SLIP.

When SLIP is employed with this extension, it allows a user to execute other TCP/IP Process/Application layer protocols (such as Telnet and FTP) over ordinary serial lines using a modem at relatively slow data transfer rates. As discussed in the section of this chapter on packet-switching, some performance loss should be expected when running a packet encapsulation protocol over slower serial lines. SLIP has received some criticism in the Internet community due to the lack of a built-in method of error detection and correction in the protocol. There is also a need for a built-in method of data compression in the protocol. The use of data compression would allow for more efficient use of serial line bandwidth, and alleviate some of the problems of using packet encapsulation at slower data rates.

At present, SLIP is not an Internet standard protocol, and is not considered part of the TCP/IP protocol suite. It was originally developed by 3COM for a UNET TCP/IP implementation in the early 1980s [RFC1055]. The protocol is available for systems using the BSD 4.3 UNIX operating system, and many variations of BSD 4.3. Although SLIP has not been adopted as an official Internet standard, it is described to the Internet community for informational purposes in RFC1055.

Talk Protocol

Talk is analogous to a written telephone conversation. The protocol is used to control the interaction of real-time communication between two terminals (two users) on the network. Both terminals can be on the same Internet host, but the talk protocol also supports terminal sessions between different hosts on the network. When a talk session is established, the words typed by one user onto her/his terminal are displayed on the terminal of the user at the other end of the connection. In implementations of talk for BSD-like UNIX operating systems, the terminal's screen is generally split into two windows (split horizontally at the 12 line). Whatever the local user types is displayed on the upper portion of the screen, and the responses from the remote user are displayed on the lower portion of the screen. The syntax of the talk application is generally:

```
<path> talk <login ID>@<address> <port>
```

where:

<path> is a directive path statement which allows the operating system to locate an executable image or file.

talk is the name of the executable program.

<login ID> is the user ID of the person with whom a connection is to be established.

<address> is the canonical name of the person's Internet host.

<port> is the Internet socket number to be used (explained under "Addressing Components"). This argument can generally be omitted from the command, and the talk default socket number of 517 will be used.

UNIX to UNIX CoPy Protocol (UUCP)

UUCP is a suite of programs for the UNIX operating system which is designed to permit communication between UNIX hosts (i.e., hosts using a UNIX-like operating system) using either dial-up or hardwired communication lines. The communication that takes place between the UNIX hosts can be file transfer, or it can be the remote execution of programs. The earliest UUCP implementations can be traced to the AT&T Bell Laboratories, the birthplace of the UNIX operating system, in the late 1970s.

The UUCP protocol should not be confused with the world-wide network that shares the name of UUCP. The name of the network itself is taken from UNIX to UNIX CoPy, which forms the foundation of data transfer on the network. The Usenet and UUNET networks are also closely affiliated with the UUCP protocol. UUCP handles the transfer of electronic mail, while network news is transferred via Usenet. The third network, UUNET, was created to relay data between UUCP, Usenet, and the Internet. Confused? Don't worry too much, so is most everyone else. (More of the interconnections among these networks and services are explained in Chapter Two.)

X.500 (and the Directory Access Protocol)

X.500 is a CCITT (Comité Consultatif International Télégraphique et Téléphonique) protocol which specifies the provision of directory services in a wide area networked environment. It is widely considered to be a viable protocol environment for the development and management of telephone and electronic mail directories in the Internet, although it is designed to also serve as a resource that other OSI application layer protocols can exploit during automated processes. A typical X.500 white pages service record would contain information such as a user's name, login ID (and full e-mail address), job title, organizational name, telephone number, and (postal) mailing address. However, X.500 is object oriented, and it provides for the construction of servers which store information related to virtually any data element imaginable. Information such as a person's favorite drink, personal hobbies, and a even a photograph of the individual (contained in a graphics format file) can also be stored in an X.500 server.

Directories built using X.500 are actually distributed databases. They function in a manner similar to that of the Berkeley Internet Name Domain (BIND) service, described earlier in this chapter. There are several advantages to this type of directory data management, the most notable of which is the fact that maintenance of directory database records is widely distributed. As new institutions add entries to the database, the directory grows larger. However, the management of the database does not increase significantly, as it would if the database were entirely centralized on one machine, because each organization is responsible for maintaining their own small subset of the database. This type of maintenance is also likely to assure that records contained within the database remain timely and accurate as changes occur.

There are two elements of an X.500 directory implementation. The Directory Service Agent (DSA) is a server (or series of hosts) that houses the database records. The Directory User Agent (DUA) is a client used to search the distributed database. Like POP clients, DUAs can be written for virtually any type of computing environment. Therefore, a DOS computer owner could use a DOS X.500 DUA, and a Macintosh owner could choose to use a Macintosh-specific DUA.

DIXIE

The X.500 protocol was designed specifically to work in the OSI environment. Because the Internet, which is based on the TCP/IP protocol suite, omits the session and presentation layers of the OSI stack there have been only a few experiments in the provision of X.500 service on the Internet thus far. Some critics argue that the additional layers of the OSI model prevent the development of DUAs for small computers such as PCs and Macintoshes because these smaller machines do not have the memory and processing capacities needed to use a full OSI stack.

As presented in RFC1249, DIXIE defines a mechanism that allows TCP- and UDP-based clients to access OSI Directory Service without using the Directory Access Protocol (DAP)—an OSI application layer. DAP requires additional protocol layers not available in the TCP/IP stack, and it is therefore considered expensive to code and maintain. DIXIE describes a method of building an X.500 client for use in the TCP/IP Internet which is intended to be usable by smaller hosts such as Macintoshes and PCs. RFC1249 provides information to the Internet community. However, it does not specify an Internet standard.

Directory Assistance Service

Another approach to the development of DUAs in the Internet is outlined in RFC1202 which describes the Directory Assistance Service developed by Performance Systems International. Like RFC1249 (DIXIE), this RFC does not specify an Internet standard, but is intended to provide information to the Internet community regarding a DAP-like implementation on TCP. In this implementation, the DUA is split into two pieces (the Directory Assistant and the DA client) in order to allow X.500 services to be developed for use on smaller machines.

Information Retrieval Service Definition and Protocol Specifications for Library Applications (Z39.50)

The Information Retrieval Service Definition and Protocol Specifications for Library Applications (Z39.50) is a protocol that defines an OSI application layer service for client/server information retrieval. Although Z39.50 is defined as an OSI application layer protocol, it can be implemented as a connection-oriented application in the TCP/IP environment. The protocol was originally published as an open standard (Z39) by the National Information Standards Organization (NISO) in 1988, although the 1988 standard has been widely criticized as being incomplete.

It has been said that a party interested in building a marketable library client/server information system using the Z39.50-1988 specification would have found that doing so was not possible without making extensions to the protocol as it was specified by NISO. For that reason, during the period between 1988 and the present, the protocol specifications have been refined and the areas where significant weaknesses were perceived have been greatly enhanced through the development of a second version of the Z39.50 standard. At the time of this writing, the second generation of the protocol (Z39.50-1992) has been distributed to NISO voting members for balloting, and it is expected to be approved without significant changes.

A critical need during the development of client/server applications is for development teams to test the inter-operation of their coded implementations (both servers and clients) against other systems. The Z39.50 Interoperability Testbed, a current project of the Coalition for Networked Information (see Chapter Five for more information on this organization), is providing support for those parties interested in the development of Z39.50-based information retrieval systems. Individuals, and organizations, interested in the implementation of Z39.50 in real and prototype systems are joined together through this project group to determine whether the 1992 revision of the protocol is sufficiently robust for wide-scale implementation. The Z39.50 Interoperability Testbed is directed by Clifford Lynch, director of library automation at University of California.

Despite the perceived weaknesses of the Z39.50-1988 protocol, there is one notable system which was prototyped based on the protocol. The Wide Area Information Server (WAIS), was jointly developed with the contributions of Thinking Machines, Apple Computer, and Dow Jones to be an information retrieval system to be used by business executives. It was prototyped, and tested in the field in the offices of Peat Marwick.

WAIS is a full-text retrieval system (using inverted indexing) which supports a client/server interface via Z39.50. It was specifically designed for users who did not want—or did not have time—to learn complexities of searching conventional text-oriented search and retrieval systems. Because there were significant weaknesses in Z39.50-1988, the WAIS implementation of Z39.50 makes the use of some substantial extensions to the protocol as it was published. Thinking Machines has made available a prototype UNIX server and a prototype Macintosh client, both of which support TCP/IP networks, in an effort to stimulate competitive development in the Z39.50 marketplace. Software developers are encouraged to use the Thinking Machines code as the basis for the development of more refined systems. More information on WAIS application(s) can be found in Chapter Four.

File Formats in the Internet

One of the greatest challenges to the development of networked information delivery applications is the wide range of data formats being used on the network. At the least, it is time consuming to build an application that will accommodate the transfer and/or translation of multiple file formats; at the worst, it is nearly impossible to accommodate all the potential file formats a user may encounter. The abundance of data formats available on the network has a direct impact on what data is available to a user. For example, if there is a paper on a topic that interests you available from a host on the network, and that paper is available only as a TeX word processing document, the information in the paper is inaccessible to you unless you have a program for your local computer(s) that can interpret the TeX markup language.

In this day and age, it is possible to process nearly any data format on your local computer (or at least to convert it into a data format that is more readily accessible) if you are persistent enough. In fact, there is a wealth of software available to perform this function. These software packages, which were often created by another network user who had a similar data translation problem at one point, are generally made available as freeware (software that the programmer gives away) or as shareware (software that the programmer asks a nominal fee for, generally in the neighborhood of $10 to $20).

However, knowing which software packages to look for requires an understanding of the type of data format at hand. On the network, data files are generally given a file extension—DOS users will be familiar with file extensions such as .EXE for executable code and .TXT for textual data—to denote their format. The two primary genres of files you are likely to encounter are text formats and binary formats. In the following sections, we will explore some commonly encountered textual and binary file formats.

Textual File Formats

The two best-known textual data formats used by hosts on the Internet are the American Standard Code for Information Interchange (ASCII) and the Extended Binary Coded Decimal Interchange Code (EBCDIC). Although many machines, most notably IBM computers, use EBCDIC for internal processing of textual information, ASCII text is widely accepted as a network standard for exchange of textual information between different hosts on the network. For this reason, nearly every computer, including IBM computers, can transmit and receive ASCII text over the network.

ASCII is a 7-bit code which was jointly developed by several computing equipment manufacturers, and is employed worldwide. EBCDIC, on the other hand, was initially developed solely by IBM, although it has been used for various tasks on many non-IBM computers. Because ASCII was designed in an effort to simplify machine-to-machine communication, it has been more widely implemented in networked environments than EBCDIC. On the network, there are two file extensions which are widely accepted to designate that a document consists of ASCII text.

These file extensions are .TXT and .ASC. By far, the .TXT representation is more common.

At this juncture, it is important to note the difference between ASCII textual data and textual data created by a word processing application such as Microsoft Word or WordPerfect. Documents created using these programs generally do *not* consist of ASCII text. Instead, in the context of network transmission, these documents should be considered binary data.

The reason for this subtle distinction is straightforward. Word processing applications create documents that contain proprietary strings of binary data in addition to the textual data itself. These proprietary strings of data are interpreted as binary data streams by the application, and contain information used by the word processing application to govern the formatting (i.e., type fonts, bold type, italic type, margins, tab stops, etc.) of the document. Although documents created using word processors are not generally saved as ASCII text, most word processors do allow users to save the document as an ASCII text document without formatting. This function allows the user to create a document that can be transmitted over the Internet, or nearly any other network for that matter, as "plain" text.

Binary File Formats

Formatted documents, program files, sounds, pictures, and full motion video, when digitized, can be transmitted across a communications channel between computers. Files consisting of these types of data are often referred to as binary data. Textual data (ASCII and EBCDIC) are based on 7- and 8-bit coding patterns, and are generally interpreted and transmitted by computers using those 7- or 8-bit coding patterns. Conversely, binary data is stored and transmitted as single binary digits (ones and zeros). This type of data storage has an advantage when being transmitted on networks, because the data can be transmitted from one host to another in the exact format in which it was stored. The interpretation of the binary data is done by the application program.

This advantage can also be viewed as a disadvantage. There is no widely accepted standard for the storage and transmission of non-textual, or binary, data. Nearly every application program available in the marketplace uses its own proprietary coding sequence for the storage of binary data. This results in an overwhelming number of binary data formats, all of which can be encountered on the network. Similarly, as programmers tackle the problem of processing an excessively large number of data formats, there are an overwhelming number of applications available to convert or interpret each of these data formats.

However, there are certain de facto file format standards being adopted for use on the network simply due to the sheer number of users who can process those file formats. Some of these file formats are listed in the table at the end of this section. The table lists the data format, the file extension commonly associated with the data format, the method of file transfer (ASCII or BINARY) to be employed when doing an FTP file transfer, and the name of an application that can be used to process or interpret the file.

Most commonly, a network traveler will encounter these various data formats when using the anonymous FTP function of an Internet host. After finding that a retrieved file has been garbled in the transmission process, a user will quickly learn to identify the format of a file by examining the tag extension appended to the filename. Files without a file extension tag can generally be assumed to be ASCII text.

The Role of Data Compression

Data files can sometimes be compressed to make them smaller. The compression of data serves several purposes. Compression of data can sometimes be used to aid in the detection and correction of errors during transmission of the file over a network. Also, since the file is smaller after it has been compressed, it consumes less space on a hard drive or a floppy disk. This can be an advantage if you have a large number of files to store on a relatively limited amount of disk storage space. Finally, and most importantly, reducing the file size also reduces the amount of time and network resources it takes to transmit a file across a communications line.

There are many different methods for compressing data files, and there are equally as many programs that can be used for compressing and extracting (restoring the data to its original size) data files. Some of the most common compression/extraction programs, and the corresponding file extensions, are shown in the table that appears in the next section. A more complete listing of known compression formats is available via anonymous FTP from the host ftp.cso.uiuc.edu (the IP is 128.174.5.59). The listing is stored as an ASCII text file called "compression" (16 Kbytes) in the directory /doc/pcnet.

A process related to data compression is Binary/Hexadecimal (BinHex) conversion. This process is most commonly employed by Macintosh computer users, although there are BinHex applications for DOS computers. BinHex is not actually used to compress files; in fact, the BinHex process frequently enlarges the size of a document. During the Binary/Hexadecimal conversion process, a binary file of some sort (e.g., a formatted word processing document, a compiled program, or a graphic image), is converted into ASCII text. This process results in a file that contains seemingly unintelligible information. Examine this segment of a bin-hexed document for example:

```
(This file must be converted with BinHex 4.0)
:#80XEh0P9QPPG`"MC'9f3P0%B5!!!!!!!!!!6-e0bJ!!!!!"!!!!5ZF!!%RR!!!
"jJ!!!!!!!!!!!!!!!!!!!!!!!!!!!!!!!!!!!!!!!!!!!!!#80XEh0P9QPPG`)!!!"
MC'9f3P0%B5%!!%!!!!!!!!!!!'0NCAC#8d4K)3!!3!!!!!!!!!!!!!!!!!!!!!!
!!!!BS5PP`!!!!!!!!%c0!!!!!!!!!!!!!!!!!!!!!!!!!!!!!!!!!!!!!!!!!!!!!!
!!!!!!!!!!!!!!!!!!!!!!!!!!!!!!!!!!!!!!!!!!!!!!!!!!!!!!!!!!!!!!!!!!!!
!!!!!!!!!!!!!!!!!!!!!!!!!!!!!!!!!!!!!!!!!!!!!!!!!!!!!!!!!!!!!!!!!!!!
!!!!!!#i"%)!!!!!$-5ia)c%Z-5`JU5""F("XC5"$Efe`GA4PFL`J5@jM,L!a16J
i,6Jj!!!!!!!!!"a#8d4K!!!!!8P$6L-!!!!!m#"'8N9'!!!!!2!J!!!"!!!!!!!
```

You may wonder why anyone would want to use this process, if it actually enlarges the size of the document before it is to be transmitted. The advantage of BinHexing a document is that such a document can be transmitted over the network as ASCII text, which is the default transfer mode on many systems. Consider a paper written in Microsoft Word for the Macintosh. If the paper is saved as ASCII text, all of the formatting will be lost. However, if the same paper is saved as in its normal format, and then converted to BinHex format, it can be easily transmitted over the network, possibly as an e-mail message. When the recipient receives it, she/he can use a Hexadecimal/Binary conversion process (also called BinHex) on the document to restore it with its original formatting intact.

Since compressed documents are always binary files, using BinHex allows a compressed file to be stored and transmitted as an ASCII file, greatly reducing the potential for errors in the process of receiving the file over the network. It is not uncommon to find documents that have been compressed and then converted to BinHex format. These files are readily identified by the fact that they possess two file extension tags, as in the examples below:

```
file1.sea.hqx
file2.cpt.hqx
```

The first file is a self-extracting archive (.sea) that has been BinHexed (.hqx). The second is a Compact Pro (.cpt) file that has been BinHexed.

Commonly Used File Formats

Data Format	File Extension	FTP Type	Application
ASCII	.asc	ascii	word processor
	.txt		word processor
Binary / Hexadecimal	.hqx	ascii	BinHex
Binary	.bin	binary	Operating System dependent
Compressed (DOS)	.ARC	binary	ARCE.COM
	.ZIP	binary	PKUNZIP.EXE
Compressed (Mac)	.cpt	binary	UnStuffit
	.sea	binary	Compact Pro
Compressed (UNIX)	.tar	binary	tape archiver
	.Z	binary	un/compress
Graphics formats	.gif	binary	Operating System dependent
	.pict	binary	Operating System dependent
	.tif/tiff	binary	Operating System dependent
Object Code	.o	binary	C (?) compiler
PostScript	.ps	ascii	Adobe PS device
Source Code (C)	.c	ascii	C compiler
Word Processing	.Word	binary	Microsoft Word
	.WP	binary	Word Perfect

Multipurpose Internet Mail Extensions (MIME)

Currently, there is a draft Internet RFC in circulation outlining a format for processing of multimedia mail messages, or composite electronic mail documents. Such an RFC, when adopted as a full Internet standard, will allow for the development of electronic mail systems able to transmit textual data, sounds, graphic images, and full motion video, in a system similar to the existing SMTP transmission of text-only files. In other words, you could record a message that included video and sound (similar to making a videotape recording of yourself talking) and send it over the TCP/IP Internet to another machine where it would be stored until the recipient was able to view it. The recipient, using a MIME compliant application, could view the message, perhaps read an accompanying textual document, and then reply to you by recording another message and sending it back to your computer.

The Multipurpose Internet Mail Extensions (MIME) Internet standard is designed to be fully compatible with existing textual based mail handlers (as defined in RFC821 and RFC822). In addition to the standard mail header fields described in RFC821 standard, the MIME-draft RFC describes a MIME version header field, a content-type header field which consists of several subfields used to describe the type(s) of data included in the body of the message, and a content transfer encoding field to specify an encoding (encryption, data compression, etc.) which may have been performed on the body of the message. The draft RFC also defines a minimal level of conformance to be used by all MIME applications.

Network Bandwidth

Once you have begun to immerse yourself in the world we know as the Internet, you are likely to hear the term "bandwidth" being used. Bandwidth refers to the range of frequencies that can be transmitted on a given communications channel. In other words, the larger the bandwidth, the wider the range of frequencies the circuit will carry, and the more data you can move over the communications channel. In the slower serial connections to which many computer users are accustomed, bandwidth is measured in the number of bits of data that can move across the circuit in a given second (bps, or baud). In packet-switched networks, bandwidth can be expressed in the number of thousands of bits per second (Kbps) or the number of packets per second that can be passed across a circuit.

Generally speaking, files in binary data formats (sounds, graphic images, and full motion video) are considerably larger than those in textual formats. Therefore, transmission of these data formats consumes a considerably greater amount of network bandwidth. The amount of bandwidth available on a given network can have a tremendous impact on the performance of Process/Application layer protocols, and may also place limitations on the types of data that can be transmitted on the network.

Some of the bandwidths employed most commonly in the myriad of networks comprising the TCP/IP Internet are shown in the table below. This chart can be misleading, however, because there are real-world implementation factors such as network use, disk-drive access, and central processor unit (CPU) bottlenecks which can make a network with a lower bandwidth channel actually outperform a network with a larger bandwidth. Additionally, transmitted signals fade (excepting fiber optics) as they cross distance due to the impedance of the copper wire. Therefore, the distance of the network link also has an impact on performance.

Network	Physical Medium	Relative Speed	Long Distance
analog w/ modem	twisted pair	300 to 19,200 bits per second	yes
56Kb serial	two pair	56 kilo (thousand) bps	yes
Apple LocalTalk	twisted pair	230.4 kilo (thousand) bps	no
10Base-T (Ethernet)	twisted pair	10 million bps	up to 100 meters
10Base-2 (Ethernet)	thinwire (coaxial)	10 million bps	up to 185 meters
10Base-5 (Ethernet)	thickwire	10 million bps	up to 500 meters
IEEE 802.3 (Ethernet)	coaxial	10 million bps	no
T1	wire cable	1.544 million bps	yes
Token Ring	coaxial	4 million bps or 16 million bps (depending on configuration)	no
T3	wire cable	45 million bps	yes
Fiber Distributed Data Interface (FDDI)	fiber optic strands	100 million bps	yes
SONET (OC12)	cable or fiber	622 million bps	yes
SONET (OC24)	cable or fiber	1.2 billion bps	yes
SONET (OC48)	cable or fiber	2.4 billion bps	yes

In 1988, the backbone(s) of the Internet was primarily made up of T1 circuits. However, the explosion in growth soon found network service providers scrambling to implement T3 circuits at the national level. By 1991, T3 circuits were installed on a significant portion of the NSFnet backbone and other mid-level regional backbones. In the period between 1988 and 1991, it wasn't even certain that TCP/IP would prove robust enough to support the 45 million bits per second at which T3 lines operate. Such concerns were unfounded, as T3 now constitutes the lion's share of backbone circuits on the Internet.

As the turn of the century approaches, and the growing number of users increases network usage, the need for even faster backbone speeds will be required to handle the increase in packet traffic. Many people believe that the next leap in network growth will come when the backbone(s) migrates to protocols such as the Synchronous Optical Networking (SONET) suite. SONET protocols will, theoretically, allow for the transmission of data on these continental circuits at the rate of several billion gigabits (billions of bits) per second. However, SONET is not the only protocol under consideration for use at the backbone level. Others include Asynchronous Transfer Mode (ATM), Frame Relay, and High Performance Parallel Interface (HPPI). All of these protocols are largely theoretical at this time.

Bandwidth in the Local Area Environment

Two decades ago, data speeds of 300 bits per second (300 baud) were fairly common, even on major circuits. More recently, 2,400 baud has become the de facto standard for serial communications links on personal computers. This standard speed has been achieved in the marketplace primarily as a result of the cost that the consumer is willing to bear. Many individuals are unwilling to pay the steep market price for modems that will enable the personal computer to operate at speeds of 4,800 baud, 9,600 baud, or even 19,200 baud. However, the 2,400 baud threshold has been crossed in the design of many institutional data systems, and 9,600 baud is generally considered a low end communication speed for many corporate applications in North America. (Recent drops in the cost of high-speed (9,600+) modems have greatly increased sales, and the de facto standard, even for individual consumers, may soon be 9,600.)

Over the Internet, access speeds of 10 megabits (millions of bits) per second are fairly common. This networking speed of 10Mbps is the basis of a series of standards for Ethernet (TCP/IP) transmission specified by the Institute of Electrical and Electronic Engineers (IEEE). The 10Base standards (10Base-5, 10Base-2, and 10Base-T) specify baseband transmission rates (only one signal on a circuit, as opposed to broadband which signifies multiple signals on a single circuit) of 10Mbps over varying lengths and types of copper wiring. The most recent of these standards, 10Base-T, allows for transmission rates of 10Mbps over conventional twisted pair (i.e., telephone lines) lines less than 100 meters in length. The 10Base-T standard is being widely employed at the local area level of the Internet throughout the world.

To the reader accustomed to data transfer rates of 2400 baud, this speed may seem incredible. Indeed, the movement of textual data on the network can be achieved quite comfortably with this speed. However, as developers in the Internet community begin to explore the delivery of multimedia information on the network through applications based on such protocols as MIME, what is considered an adequate speed today may be considered insufficient or unnecessarily restrictive tomorrow. If we expect to see distributed library applications that will routinely search, retrieve, and present multi-media objects on the network, we must consider significantly greater bandwidths at the local level as a precursor to such systems.

Our Parting Shot

We hope that you have found the material in this chapter informative. Obviously, a great deal of material included was only addressed in the briefest possible manner. Nevertheless, we hope to have given an introduction to some new concepts that are intimately related to the TCP/IP Internet. To check our effectiveness, we thought we would include this offering from one of the founding fathers of inter-networking, Vinton Cerf. If you find this to be somewhat amusing, or if you are not completely befuddled by it, then we believe this chapter has accomplished its purpose.

Rosencrantz and Ethernet
by Vint Cerf

All the world's a net! And all the data in it merely packets
Come to store-and-forward in the queues a while and then are
Heard no more. 'Tis a network waiting to be switched!

To switch or not to switch? That is the question. Whether
'Tis wiser in the net to suffer the store and forward of
Stochastic networks or to raise up circuits against a sea
Of packets and, by dedication, serve them.

To net, to switch. To switch, perchance to slip!
Aye, there's the rub. For in that choice of switch,
What loops may lurk, when we have shuffled through
This Banyan net? Puzzles the will, initiates symposia,
Stirs endless debate and gives rise to uncontrolled
Flights of poetry beyond recompense!

Chapter Four: Network Applications

This chapter provides an introduction to some of the major application software programs used on the Internet. Applications are the programs that allow you to send electronic mail messages and files to other network users, to retrieve files stored at other sites, and to access resources across the network.

We have provided explanations of some of the different types of applications available, along with examples of some of the most commonly used versions of these programs from a variety of operating system perspectives. However, since implementations of application software can vary substantially from one computer system to the next, it is important that you consult documentation for your local system (or consult a computer support staff person for your system) before using any of these programs on your own computer.

Electronic Mail

Electronic mail is the most commonly used and well-known application on the Internet. Electronic mail allows network users to send messages to each other. The speed that electronic delivery affords makes this method of communication very attractive. Like the facsimile machine, electronic mail has made it possible for substantive communication to take place quickly and easily over both time and distance.

Unlike the telephone system, however, electronic mail does not yet have a consistent and well-documented method for assigning addresses. Although progress has been made in making electronic mail communication between Internet hosts more intuitive and less confusing, there is still a long way to go before using electronic mail is as easy as using the telephone. The more you know about the interconnections among machines, and about the electronic mail applications available, the easier it will be for you to make the most of your e-mail connection.

In Chapter Three, we looked at some of the technical concepts underlying electronic mail-addressing conventions, Simple Mail Transfer Protocol (SMTP), and some of the mail-related Requests for Comments (RFCs). In this section, we look at the practical application of electronic mail in a variety of environments.

Mailer Programs

The mailer program is your interface to the electronic mail system. There are a variety of mailer programs available for both host and desktop systems, and the diversity of programs makes it difficult—if not impossible—to write a single "how-to" guide for electronic mail. For information on using the mailer program on your local system, contact your system or network administrator.

If you have Phase One or Phase Two connectivity, you are not likely to have a choice as to which mailer you use. Typically, a host system has only one or two mailer programs available for its users. The system administrator (or computer center) decides which mailer program will best suit the needs of users (taking into account budgetary and system constraints), and often customizes the program for the local host.

The majority of large Internet hosts are either IBM (or IBM-compatible) mainframes, or UNIX™-based minicomputers. On the IBM, two commonly used mailer programs are Rice Mailbook and PROFS. On the VAX, UNIX™ programs include Extended Berkeley Mailer, elm, and Z-Mail; on VAX/VMS systems, the VMS Mail utility is often used.

If you have desktop connectivity, the mail options available to you are more extensive, and also more customizable. Most electronic mail packages currently being used on local area networks have the capability to be adapted to Internet access. There are also packages available that are designed specifically for Internet e-mail on personal computers.

If your local network or computer is connected to the Internet (Phase Three connectivity), the software can be configured to send your messages directly to your recipient. If your network is using a connection to another host system (Phase One or Phase Two connectivity), your system administrator will need to install "gateway" software.

Finding Addresses

There is no single, up-to-date, comprehensive listing of electronic mail addresses. And to complicate matters, there is not even one standard format for individual addresses. There are a number of books and network resources that can be used to find someone's electronic mail address, and those resources are described in this section. However, there is one method of finding electronic mail addresses that is more reliable than any described below: calling the person for whom you need an electronic mail address and asking them for it.

WHOIS Servers

The WHOIS database is an interactive program that allows network users to register their names and electronic mail addresses, and to search for information on other network users. It includes information about hosts and domains as well as users. The best-known implementation of this program is the QUIPU WHOIS database maintained by the network information center for the DDN (Defense Data Network). The QUIPU WHOIS database can be accessed by running a WHOIS client program from a remote host, by Telneting to nic.ddn.mil and running the WHOIS program interactively, or by sending a database query to the server via e-mail. Help on using the QUIPU WHOIS server can be obtained by sending an electronic mail message with the word "help" in the message text to service@nic.ddn.mil. (WHOIS databases are implented using the X.500 protocol described in Chapter Three.)

If you have some information about an Internet host's domain (see Chapter Three for more information on host names and domains), WHOIS can be used to search for more complete information. Locating the domain or network record will provide an informational address for that system.

A list of WHOIS servers at other sites has been collected and compiled by Matt Power of MIT. The list is available via FTP from sipb.mit.edu. The filename and location are: /pub/whois/whois-servers.list.

Below is a transcript of a WHOIS session conducted on a local host that runs a version of the client software.

In the first query, the nic.ddn.mil database is accessed and searched for the term "coalition".

```
a.cni.org> whois -h nic.ddn.mil coalition
Coalition for Networked Information (CNI-DOM)   CNI.ORG
Coalition for Networked Information (NET-CNI)
CNI   192.100.21.0

To single out one record, look it up with "!xxx", where xxx is
the handle, shown in parenthesis following the name, which comes
first.
```

This search yields a result for the Coalition for Networked Information (CNI). With the information on the domain name (shown in parentheses following the name, as noted in the information on the screen), we can search for more detailed information on CNI. The following query also searches in the nic.ddn.mil database, this time with the specific domain name CNI-DOM.

```
a.cni.org> whois -h nic.ddn.mil CNI-DOM
Coalition for Networked Information (CNI-DOM)
   1527 New Hampshire Avenue, NW
   Washington, D.C. 20036

Domain Name: CNI.ORG

Administrative Contact:
 Peters, Paul Evan (PEP2) paul@cni.org
 (202) 232-2466
Technical Contact, Zone Contact:
 Summerhill, Craig A. (CAS85) craig@cni.org
 (202) 232-2466

Record last updated on 13-Apr-92.

Domain servers in listed order:

A.CNI.ORG        192.100.21.1
NOC.SURA.NET     192.80.214.100
```

To see this host record with registered users, repeat the command with a star ('*') before the name; or, use '%' to show JUST the registered users.

This more detailed information gives the primary contacts for CNI's host machine. It is also possible to look for information on individual users, as below:

```
a.cni.org> whois -h nic.ddn.mil summerhill
Summerhill, Craig A. (CAS85)  craig@cni.org
(202) 232-2466
Summerhill, Richard R. (RRS31) RRSUM@HERMZEL.KSU.KSU.EDU
(913) 532-6750

To single out one record, look it up with "!xxx", where xxx is
the handle, shown in parenthesis following the name, which comes
first.
```

This search yields two matches on the name "summerhill." Again, the information at the bottom of the screen tells how to find more detailed information on one of those names by using the unique identifier following the name.

```
a.cni.org> whois -h nic.ddn.mil CAS85
Summerhill, Craig A. (CAS85)  craig@cni.org
   Coalition for Networked Information
   1527 New Hampshire Ave., N.W.
   Washington, D.C. 20036
   (202) 232-2466

Record last updated on 13-Apr-92.
```

Usenet Addresses Server

A database of Usenet participants is maintained on the pit-manager.mit.edu host. This database contains the addresses of anyone who has posted a message to a Usenet newsgroup.

To query the database, send a message to

```
mail-server@pit-manager.mit.edu
```

with the text:

```
send Usenet-addresses/name
```

in the body or subject of the message, where *name* is either the first or last name of the person whose address you are seeking.

Non-alphabetic characters in names (such as apostrophes) should be replaced with a period (e.g., o.brien). The database is not case-sensitive, so the name can appear in upper- or lower-case letters.

You can send more than one request in the same message, but each request must appear on a separate line of the message. Each request will result in a separate message from the mail server.

The database is also available using the WAIS software described in the "Advanced Applications" section of this chapter. It can be searched via WAIS on two hosts: pit-manager.mit.edu and cedar.cic.net. In both cases, the database is called "Usenet-addresses."

Usenet Files and Newsgroups

There are a number of files maintained by Usenet newsgroups that can be helpful in finding the addresses of Usenet participants. Since many Internet, BITNET, and even FidoNet sites provide access to Usenet newsgroups, these postings may also be useful in finding the addresses of people on a variety of network hosts.

The files listed below are available via anonymous FTP from the Usenet file archive at pit-manager.mit.edu (18.72.1.58). They can also be requested using an electronic mail-based file service. For more information on the mail-based service, send a message containing the word "help" to mail-server@pit-manager.mit.edu.

The soc.college newsgroup maintains a file called "College E-mail Addresses." This file describes the e-mail account and address policies for students at many colleges and universities. It also provides information on how to get more help on addresses from the individual institutions. This file is also available through the soc.net-people and comp.mail.misc newsgroups, described below.

The comp.mail.misc newsgroup focuses primarily on technical and mechanical aspects of electronic mail, including mailer software and addressing conventions. However, because questions about finding addresses occur so often, they maintain the following files in the /pub/Usenet/comp.mail.misc subdirectory:

```
Inter-Network_Mail_Guide
FAQ:_How_to_find_people_s_E-mail_addresses
```

As a last resort, the soc.net-people newsgroup can be used for queries like "Does anyone out there know Person X, and whether she/he can be reached by electronic mail?" Before posting a message to soc.net-people, be sure to read their file "Tips on using soc.net-people." In the /pub/Usenet/soc.net-people subdirectory are the following files:

```
Tips_on_using_soc.net-people
College_Email_Addresses
Internet_Services_List
FAQ:_College_Email_Addresses_1_2_[Monthly_posting].part1
FAQ:_College_Email_Addresses_1_2_[Monthly_posting].part2
FAQ:_College_Email_Addresses_2_2_[Monthly_posting]
```

BITNET Name Servers

Several BITNET sites maintain user directory servers, with listings of local participants. In many cases, remote users can register their names with these name servers.

To search a BITNET NAMESERV server, BITNET users can send an interactive message (using the TELL or SEND commands). Internet users can query most servers through e-mail messages.

As an example, an interactive search on the Drew University NAMESERV is illustrated below.

On a VM/CMS system, type the command:

```
TELL NAMESERV AT DREW SEARCH/NAME Jane Doe
```

On a VMS/JNET system, type the command:

```
SEND NAMESERV@DREW "SEARCH/NAME Jane Doe"
```

A list of NAMESERV hosts is included in the BITNET SERVERS document, which is available via FTP from several archive sites. To retrieve information on searching a specific NAMESERV, send an e-mail message to:

```
NAMESERV@NODE.BITNET.
```

with the word "help" in the body of the message.

One user directory server that allows remote users to register themselves is NAMESERV@DREW. Information on registering is available using the HELP command in an interactive or e-mail message. The interactive registration process is illustrated below:

On a VM/CMS system:

```
TELL NAMESERV AT DREW REGISTER first last keywords
```

On a VMS/JNET system:

```
SEND NAMESERV@DREW "REGISTER first last keywords"
```

BITNET LISTSERV Participant Lists

It is possible to retrieve a list of participants and their e-mail addresses from a LISTSERV server (for more information on LISTSERVs, see the "Mailing Lists/ Electronic Conferences" section of this chapter).

To receive the list from a specific LISTSERV conference, send the LISTSERV at that site a message with the words "REV *conference*", where *conference* is the name of the conference, in the text of the message. For example, to retrieve the participant list for the PACS-L conference on UHUPVM1 at the University of Houston, you would send the message to

```
LISTSERV@UHUPVM1.BITNET
```

with the text:

```
REV PACS-L
```

in the body of the message. (No subject heading is necessary.) The LISTSERV will send you the file. If you send the message from a BITNET address, you will receive the file in NETDATA format, sent directly to your readerlist of files. If you send the message from a non-BITNET address, you will receive the file via electronic mail.

You can then search the file for a particular user or institution. (If you expect to search the list regularly, you may wish to download the file directly to your desktop computer, and search it using word processing software.)

Books

It can be difficult to decipher the electronic mail addresses of other network users. An address that takes one form on a BITNET host will take a different form on an Internet host. Sending mail to systems that provide gateways to the network often have special addressing conventions. In addition to the information provided in Chapter Three of this book, the books listed below can be helpful in identifying the network that a correspondent uses, and in finding the correct address form for that host computer.

Frey, D., & Adams, R. (1990). *!%@: A directory of electronic mail addressing and networks.* (Sebastopol, CA: O'Reilly and Associates).

La Quey, T. L. (1990). *The user's directory of computer networks.* (Bedford, MA: Digital Press).

Quarterman, J. S. (1990). *The matrix: computer networks and conferencing systems worldwide.* (Bedford, MA: Digital Press).

Electronic Mail Etiquette

Electronic mail is a relatively new method of communication. Its benefits are obvious; communication can take place quickly and inexpensively. However, because with e-mail non-verbal clues like tone of voice and expression are lost, guidelines for communicating electronically have developed in the network community.

Etiquette Primer

A guide designed for Usenet newsgroup participants is "A Primer on How to Work With the USENET Community," by Chuq Von Rospach (the original file is available from a number of FTP sites, including ftp.uu.net and pit-manager.mit.edu). Although these tips were originally written for Usenet users, the selected items below are easily applicable to electronic mail.

- **Never forget the person on the other side is human.**
  Because your interaction with the network is through a computer it is easy to forget that there are people "out there." Situations arise where emotions erupt into a verbal free-for-all that can lead to hurt feelings.

  If you are upset at something or someone, wait until you have had a chance to calm down and think about it. A cup of coffee or a good night's sleep works wonders on your perspective. Hasty words create more problems than they solve. Try not to say anything to others you would not say to them in person.

- **Be careful with humor and sarcasm.**
Without the voice inflections and body language of personal communications, it is easy for a remark meant to be funny to be misinterpreted. Subtle humor tends to get lost, so take steps to make sure that people realize you are trying to be funny. Network users have developed a symbol called the smiley face. It looks like ":-)" and points out sections of articles with humorous intent. No matter how broad the humor or satire, it is safer to remind people that you are being funny.

    But also be aware that quite frequently satire is posted without any explicit indications. If an article outrages you strongly, you should ask yourself if it just may have been unmarked satire. Several self-proclaimed connoisseurs refuse to use smiley faces, so take heed or you may make a temporary fool of yourself.

- **Don't overdo signatures.**
Signatures are nice, and many people can have a signature added to their postings automatically by placing it in a file called "$HOME/.signature". Don't overdo it. Signatures can tell the world something about you, but keep them short. A signature that is longer than the message itself is considered to be in bad taste. The main purpose of a signature is to help people locate you, not to tell your life story. Every signature should include at least your return address relative to a major, known site on the network and a proper domain-format address. Your system administrator can give this to you. Some news posters attempt to enforce a four-line limit on signature files—an amount that should be more than sufficient to provide a return address and attribution.

- **Limit line length and avoid control characters.**
Try to keep your text in a generic format. Many (if not most) of the people reading Usenet do so from eighty-column terminals or from workstations with eighty-column terminal windows. Try to keep your lines of text to less than eighty characters for optimal readability. Also realize that there are many, many different forms of terminals in use. If you enter special control characters in your message, it may result in your message being unreadable on some terminal types; a character sequence that causes reverse video on your screen may result in a keyboard lock and graphics mode on someone else's terminal. You should also try to avoid the use of tabs, since they may also be interpreted differently on terminals other than your own.

Smiley Faces

Von Rospach's primer mentions the use of smileys to indicate tone and expression in a message. A few commonly used smileys are shown below. (If they don't look like faces to you, try turning the page 45° clockwise.)

:-)   Your basic smiley.

;-)   Winking smiley. Usually denotes sarcasm.

}-)   Evil smiley.

:-}   Wry smiley.

:-(Frowning smiley.

:-0   Surprised or exclaiming smiley.

%-)   User has been staring at a computer screen for 15 hours.

Mailing Lists/Electronic Conferences

Mailing lists—also known as electronic conferences—provide a way for network users sharing an interest in a given topic to exchange messages to an entire group. With a mailing list, a participant can send a message to a central address, and the message is then rebroadcast to all other participants. With some mailing lists, incoming messages are screened by a moderator before being sent out. Other, "unmoderated" mailing lists immediately rebroadcast all incoming messages.

There are hundreds of electronic conferences on the networks, covering a range of topics from computer science to library science to zoology. To keep track of all these conferences, several "lists of lists" have been created, and are updated regularly.

Editorial Control of Mailing Lists

The degree of editorial control of mailing lists varies greatly from one list to another. At the least-controlled end of the spectrum are unmoderated, unedited conferences that rebroadcast all postings from all users, and have no restrictions on participation. The majority of Usenet newsgroups fall into this category, as do many of the BITNET and Internet mailing lists.

The next level of control is the involvement of a one or more list moderators or editors (also called "owners") who receive messages that are sent to the list, and screen them for appropriateness to the forum. At times, they will reject a message or edit it for brevity. On some lists, they will combine similar messages on a given topic into a single posting. The degree of control exerted over which messages are posted is minimal, and the moderator/editor generally tries to play an unobtrusive role.

From moderated lists, the next step is to "digests." In this form, most commonly used in high-traffic mailing lists, the moderator or editor compiles all messages for a single time period (most often a day) into a single message, which is then sent to the participants. This cuts down on message traffic, and makes it easier for participants to download and read the files at leisure.

Finally, at the high end of the spectrum, there is the newsletter format. This is similar to the digest, but with a greater degree of editorial control. Where the digest editor weeds out occasional messages and sends on the rest, the newsletter editor selects only what are, in her/his opinion, the best messages sent to the list.

BITNET LISTSERVs

Revised LISTSERV is a software package for IBM BITNET hosts that was developed and is copyrighted by Eric Thomas. Although the LISTSERV software is best-known for its ability to manage mailing lists, it has other capabilities. LISTSERV servers can be used to maintain searchable databases, and to archive files and deliver them to users upon request.

When you subscribe to a BITNET list, you will receive a message containing some basic information on how to use the LISTSERV features. There are also several good guides to using LISTSERVs that are available over the network. One is "A Resource Guide to Listservers, BITNET, Internet, and Usenet," by Dennis W. Viehland of the University of Arizona. It is available from the LISTSERV at ARIZVM1, with the filename LISTSERV GUIDE (see "Retrieving Files," below, for instructions on retrieving this or other files from LISTSERVs).

Subscribing

The form of a LISTSERV list name takes the form of the list title and the BITNET node that houses it. Some examples of list names are PACS-L@UHUPVM1 and CDROMLAN@IDBSU.

Once you have obtained the name of the list to which you would like to subscribe, you need to send a message to the LISTSERV at the appropriate BITNET site, *not* to the list itself. For example, to subscribe to PACS-L, you would send the following message to:

```
LISTSERV@UHUPVM1.BITNET
```

with the text:

```
SUBSCRIBE PACS-L YourFirstName YourLastName
```

in the body of the message. (No subject is necessary; the LISTSERV software will ignore the subject line.)

Use the form of your name that you would like to have appear in the LISTSERV participant list. The LISTSERV software will extract your actual electronic mail address from the return address on the message.

You will receive a confirmation message from the LISTSERV, as well as a general introduction to LISTSERV lists, via e-mail.

All administrative messages—to subscribe, retrieve files, or search databases—should be sent to the LISTSERV itself (e.g., LISTSERV@UHUPVM1.BITNET), rather than to themailing list (e.g., PACS-L@UHUPVM1.BITNET) address.

Reading and Sending Messages

Once you have become a subscriber to the list, you will begin receiving messages from the LISTSERV on a regular basis. The volume of message traffic varies greatly from one list to another. In addition, messages from unmoderated lists can arrive at any time, depending only on technical aspects of processing and delivery times.

Messages from moderated lists tend to arrive in batches, as the moderator(s) will screen the messages for a day (or more) and then rebroadcast them together.

To send a new message to a LISTSERV mailing list, address the message to LISTNAME@NODE.BITNET. For example, a message intended for the PACS-L list would be sent to:

```
PACS-L@UHUPVM1.BITNET
```

LISTSERV messages are sent in standard electronic mail format; you can read messages, save them, and respond to them in the same way you do other electronic mail messages.

There is one important caveat to keep in mind when responding to mailing list messages. Although a message may show the name and address of the original author in the "From" field, responding directly will result in your reply being sent to the list, not to the original author. On an unmoderated list, your reply (which may be quite personal) will then be automatically rebroadcast to all list participants.

If your electronic mail system shows the full header information for a record, you may be able to differentiate between the "From" and the "Reply-to" fields. The first is the original author of the message; the second is the address to which your reply will be sent. Some mailers allow replies that go directly to the "From" address rather than defaulting to the "Reply-to" address. It is safest, however, to always send personal mail directly to the recipient, rather than replying to a mailing list message.

Searching LISTSERV Databases

One of the most powerful features of the LISTSERV software is its ability to maintain databases of list messages that are searchable by network users. These databases can be searched interactively by BITNET users, or through e-mail requests from any network user. We provide a brief introduction to searching LISTSERV databases in this section; for a more in-depth guide, send an e-mail message to any LISTSERV (LISTSERV@NODE) with the text "INFO DATABASE" in the body of the message.

Interactive database searching is described in the longer database guide mentioned above. In this section, we will discuss the batch mode method of searching, which allows searching via electronic mail messages.

The syntax used to search the databases is from a programming language for IBM mainframe computer. Its is quite arcane and not at all intuitive. To simplify the process of searching, many users create "template" messages with the database searching commands, and then modify these messages with the new search parameters each time they query a LISTSERV database.

In this example, the database of messages is used from the PACS-L mailing list, which is maintained at the UHUPVM1 BITNET node. The e-mail message will be sent to the LISTSERV processor at that node (LISTSERV@UHUPVM1, or listserv@uhupvm1.bitnet), rather than to the list itself.

Let's suppose we remember hearing about a new journal on hypertext and hypermedia, and want to find any references to it on PACS-L. The text we will search for in the database is the word "hypertext." This search should retrieve a list of all messages that mention the word. The message should have a blank subject line, and should contain the following text:

```
//
Database Search DD=Rules
//Rules DD  *
Search hypertext in PACS-L
Index
/*
```

(The text appearing in italics will vary based on which database is being queried, and which topic is being researched.)

The LISTSERV will return two pieces of information. The first will be an e-mail message providing information on the status of the request, and the amount of processing time required to process it. The second will be the actual output file, which will be called DATABASE OUTPUT. For this sample search, the output file would contain the following information:

```
> Search Hypertext in PACS-L
—> Database PACS-L, 137 hits.
```

```
> Index
Item #    Date        Time     Recs   Subject
———       ——          ——       ——     ———-
000022    89/06/30    08:31    306    Common Knowledge Info.
000047    89/07/07    08:15    18     Hypertext Conference
000075    89/07/12    17:13    21     Hypertext & Hypermedia Arti-
                                      cles
000088    89/07/13    16:19    17     CD-ROM Expo '89
000194    89/07/22    14:11    25     Hyperdoc
000248    89/07/30    20:00    23     Hypertext Hands-On!
000251    89/07/31    12:52    14     Re: Hypertext Hands-On!
000253    89/07/31    15:04    47     Was: Hypertext Hands-On!
000267    89/08/03    09:38    24     A New Journal — Hypermedia
000311    89/08/11    12:18    23     Hypermedia & Optical Tech.
                                      Resources
000338    89/08/17    11:37    33     Hypermedia/Multimedia
[The rest of the list is omitted.]
```

Based on this information, we may choose to view the entire text of one of the messages. In this case, message number 267 appears to describe the journal we're looking for. We now prepare a second message for the LISTSERV containing the following text:

```
//
Database Search DD=Rules
//Rules DD  *
```

```
Search hypertext in PACS-L
Print all of 267
/*
```

Again, the LISTSERV returns both an e-mail message and the output file, which contains the text of the requested PACS-L message. The output file looks like this:

```
> Search hypertext in PACS-L
-> Database PACS-L, 137 hits.

> Print all of 267
>>> Item number 267, dated 89/08/03 09:38:14 - ALL
[The retrieved message is here.]
```

To print multiple messages, just add the additional numbers:

```
Print all of 267 311
```

The Boolean AND operator is implicit:

```
Search hypertext journal in PACS-L
```

To make search logic clearer, the AND operator can be explicit, as well:

```
Search hypertext AND journal in PACS-L
```

The Boolean OR operator must be explicitly specified:

```
Search hypertext OR hypermedia in PACS-L
```

The Boolean NOT operator must also be explicitly specified:

```
Search hypertext NOT hypercard in PACS-L
```

Parentheses can be used to nest terms and operators:

```
Search (hypertext OR hypermedia) AND journal in PACS-L
```

Retrieving Files

LISTSERVs have the capability to store files, and to send files to users upon request. Because commands for file retrieval can vary from server to server, the first command to issue to a LISTSERV before requesting files is the HELP command, which is accepted by nearly all servers. Sending a message to LISTSERV@*NODE* where *NODE* is the BITNET location of the server, with the word "help" as the message text, will generally result in a message or a file with instructions being sent to your account.

For most LISTSERV file servers, a list of files can be requested by sending the server a message with the command INDEX or DIR in the message text. The list of files will then be sent to you as a message or a file.

Unsubscribing

To stop receiving mail from a BITNET LISTSERV mailing list, you need to send a message to the LISTSERV at the appropriate BITNET site, *not* to the list itself. For example, to unsubscribe to PACS-L, you would send the following message to:

        LISTSERV@UHUPVM1.BITNET

with the text:

        UNSUBSCRIBE PACS-L

in the body of the message. (No subject is necessary.)

You need not include your name in this command; the LISTSERV extracts your ID from the return address of the message. As a result, you can only send an unsubscribe request from the account on which you originally subscribed. If that is not possible, you will need to contact the list owner to have your name removed manually. List owner names generally appear on the participant list, which can be retrieved following the directions under "Finding Addresses" earlier in this chapter.

If you know you will be out of town and unable to read your e-mail, you may wish to temporarily stop receiving messages without removing yourself from the conference. (This is especially useful in high-traffic conferences, which can overload your mailbox if you are away for a period of time.) To do this, send the an e-mail message to LISTSERV@*NODE* with the text: SET *ListName* NOMAIL.

To resume mail delivery upon your return, send an e-mail message to the same LISTSERV@*NODE* address with the text: SET PACS-L MAIL.

Internet Mailing Lists

Unlike the LISTSERV mailing lists, Internet mailing lists do not all use a standard command format for joining or participating.

Instructions on subscribing to individual mailing lists are provided in an extensive list of scholarly conferences, called the "Directory of Scholarly Electronic Conferences," created and maintained by Diane Kovacs (DKOVACS@KENTVM). The file is described in more detail in the "Lists of Mailing Lists" section in Chapter Five.

Newsgroups (Usenet)

The bulletin board structure of Usenet is based on a large number of discussion categories called newsgroups. Each individual contribution, or posting, to a newsgroup is called an article. A broad spectrum of topics is covered by the variety of newsgroups, including technical, recreational and cultural issues, hobbies, announcements, and current events. In 1983 there were nearly 100 newsgroups and today there are about 500 newsgroups distributed nationally.

Not all Usenet sites receive all newsgroups; while some newsgroups reach an international audience others are restricted to a certain country, region, organization or even to the users of a single machine. Due to space considerations, any particular article is usually held at a site for a only a limited amount of time, and this time window is variable and determined by a site's individual policies. A number of newsgroups are moderated, and some are in digest form.

Usenet has several advantages over mailing list format. First, all messages for a group are received only once by a site, rather than by multiple users. This cuts down on the amount of network bandwidth used, as well as the amount of local storage space an individual user must have. In addition, Usenet news reading software generally has features that can speed the reading and processing of individual articles; "kill files," for example, which allows users to specify topics or keywords for messages they do not wish to read.

The Usenet system uses a hierarchical classification system to name its discussion groups. The groups distributed worldwide are divided into seven broad classifications: "comp", "sci", "misc", "soc", "talk", "news", and "rec". Each of these classifications is organized into groups and subgroups according to topic.

comp

The comp newsgroups cover topics of interest to both computer professionals and hobbyists, including computer science, software source, and information on hardware and software systems. Within the comp classification, there are breakdowns for individual computer systems, and within those, for specific computer topics. Some examples of comp newsgroups are:

comp.edu	Computer science education.
comp.lang.fortran	Discussions about FORTRAN.
comp.lang.pasca	Discussions about Pascal.
comp.mail.misc	General discussions about computer mail.
comp.os.misc	General OS-oriented discussions not carried elsewhere.
comp.os.research	Operating systems and related areas. (Moderated)
comp.os.vms	DEC's VAX™ line of computers and VMS.
comp.society	The impact of technology on society. (Moderated)
comp.society.futures	Events in technology affecting future computing.
comp.sources.wanted	Requests for software and fixes.
comp.sys.amiga.games	Discussions of games for the Commodore Amiga.
comp.sys.ibm.pc.digest	The IBM PC, PC-XT, and PC-AT. (Moderated)
comp.sys.mac.hardware	Macintosh hardware issues and discussions.
comp.sys.next	NeXT's workstations, peripherals, and software.
comp.unix	Discussions of UNIX™ features and bugs. (Moderated)
comp.windows.misc	Various issues about windowing systems.

sci

The sci newsgroups include discussions intended as technical in nature and relating to the established sciences. Sci groups include:

sci.aeronautics	The science of aeronautics and related technology.
sci.math	Mathematical discussions and pursuits.
sci.math.stat	Statistics discussions.
sci.physics	Physical laws, properties, etc.
sci.physics.fusion	Information on fusion, especially "cold" fusion.
sci.psychology.digest	Psychology discussions and information. (Moderated)

misc

The misc newsgroups address themes not easily classified under any of the other headings, or topics that incorporate themes from multiple categories. Some examples of misc groups are:

misc.consumers	Consumer interests, product reviews, etc.
misc.education	Discussions of the educational system.
misc.fitness	Physical fitness, exercise, etc.
misc.forsale	Short, tasteful postings about items for sale.
misc.rural	Devoted to issues concerning rural living.
misc.wanted	Requests for things that are needed. (NOT software)

soc

The soc groups were created to address social issues and socializing. Among the current soc groups are the following:

soc.college	College, college activities, campus life, etc.
soc.culture.greek	Group about Greeks.
soc.culture.japan	Everything Japanese, except the Japanese language.
soc.culture.jewish	Jewish culture and religion.
soc.feminism	Feminism and feminist issues. (Moderated)
soc.religion.christian	Christianity and related topics. (Moderated)
soc.religion.eastern	Discussions of Eastern religions. (Moderated)
soc.religion.islam	Discussions of the Islamic faith. (Moderated)
soc.singles	Newsgroup for single people, activities, etc.

talk

The talk groups are largely debate-oriented and tend to feature long discussions on controversial topics. Some current talk groups include:

talk.abortion	Discussions and arguments on abortion.
talk.bizarre	The unusual, bizarre, curious, and often stupid.
talk.politics.guns	The politics of firearm ownership and (mis)use.
talk.politics.mideast	Discussions and debates over Middle Eastern events.
talk.politics.misc	Political discussions and ravings of all kinds.
talk.religion.misc	Religious, ethical, and moral implications.
talk.religion.newage	Esoteric and minority religions and philosophies.
talk.rumors	For the postings of rumors.

news

The news groups are concerned with the Usenet news network and news reading software. Some news groups currently available are:

news.admin	Comments directed to news administrators.
news.announce.newusers	Explanatory postings for new users. (Moderated)
news.groups	Discussions and lists of newsgroups.
news.lists	News-related statistics and lists. (Moderated)
news.misc	Discussions of Usenet itself.
news.newsites	Postings of new site announcements.
news.newusers.questions	Questions and answers for users new to the Usenet.

rec

The rec newsgroups are for discussion of hobbies and recreational activities. Some current rec newsgroups include:

rec.arts.books	Books of all genres, and the publishing industry.
rec.arts.movies	Discussions of movies and movie making.
rec.food.cooking	Food, cooking, cookbooks, and recipes.
rec.food.drink	Wines and spirits.
rec.games.go	Discussions about Go.
rec.games.misc	Games and computer games.
rec.humor	Jokes and the like. May be somewhat offensive.
rec.humor.funny	Jokes that are funny (in the moderator's opinion). (Moderated)
rec.music.makers	For performers and their discussions.
rec.music.misc	Music lovers' group.
rec.music.newage	"New Age" music discussions.
rec.sport.baseball	Discussions about baseball.
rec.sport.misc	Spectator sports.

Gatewayed Newsgroups

Some BITNET mailing lists are also provided in Usenet form. For mailing lists with large numbers of messages, the Usenet news reader can be a more efficient tool for keeping up with a mailing list than the traditional electronic mail distribution.

Newsgroups that have been gatewayed from BITNET begin with the "bit" designation, and are followed by the name of the BITNET list. For example, PACS-L is gatewayed to Usenet as bit.pacs-l.

Alternative Usenet Hierarchies

There are also some Usenet hierarchies that are not part of the "traditional" Usenet structure, but are made available through the same mechanism as the hierarchies described above. These groups are available to sites wishing to support them, but are not carried by many sites because of space restrictions, lack of interest by a given site, or concerns about content.

alt

The alt hierarchy is a small collection of newsgroups which are considered "alternative" topics, and are carried by a limited number of sites. Some newsgroups in this category include:

alt.activism	Activities for activists.
alt.censorship	Discussions about restricting speech/press.
alt.cyberpunk	High-tech low-life.
alt.fan.dave_barry	Electronic fan club for humorist Dave Barry.
alt.folklore.urban	Urban legends, ala Jan Harold Brunvand.
alt.recovery	For people in recovery programs (e.g., AA, ACA).
alt.religion.computers	People who believe computing is "real life."
alt.sex	Postings of a prurient nature.
alt.skinheads	The skinhead culture/anti-culture.
alt.stupidity	Discussions about stupid newsgroups.
alt.tv.simpsons	Don't have a cow, man!
alt.tv.twin-peaks	Discussions about the popular (and unusual) TV show.

bionet

The bionet hierarchy contains topics of interest to biologists. The newsgroups originate from the genbank.bio.net site, and are being carried on a growing number of machines. Contact Eliot Lear <usenet@genbank.bio.net> for more details. Some current bionet newsgroups include:

bionet.agroforestry	Discussions of Agroforestry.
bionet.general	General BIONET announcements.
bionet.jobs	Scientific job opportunities.
bionet.journals.contents	Contents of biology journals.
bionet.molbio.embldatabank	Information about the EMBL Nucleic acid database
bionet.molbio.evolution	How genes and proteins have evolved.
bionet.molbio.genome-program	Discussions of Human Genome Project.
bionet.molbio.news	Research news of interest to the community.
bionet.population-bio	Technical discussions on population biology
bionet.sci-resources	Information on funding agencies, etc.
bionet.software	Information on software for biology.
bionet.users.addresses	Who's who in biology.

biz

The biz hierarchy of newsgroups focuses on business products—in particular, computer products and services. This includes product announcements, announcements of fixes and enhancements, product reviews, and postings of demo software. Current biz groups include:

biz.clarinet	Announcements about ClariNet.
biz.clarinet.sample	Samples of ClariNet newsgroups.
biz.comp.hardware	Generic commercial hardware postings.
biz.comp.services	Generic commercial service postings.
biz.comp.software	Generic commercial software postings.
biz.comp.telebit	Support of the Telebit modem.
biz.dec	DEC equipment and software.
biz.dec.workstations	DEC workstation discussions and information.
biz.jobs.offered	Position announcements.
biz.misc	Miscellaneous commercial postings.
biz.stolen	Postings about stolen merchandise.

clari

The ClariNet hierarchy consists of newsgroups gatewayed from commercial news services and other "official" sources. A feed of the ClariNet groups requires payment of a fee and execution of a license. More information may be obtained by sending mail to "info@clarinet.com". Some Clarinet newsgroups include:

clari.news	ClariNet UPI general news.
clari.news.hot	Temporary groups for hot news stories.
clari.biz	ClariNet UPI business news.
clari.sports	ClariNet UPI sports.
clari.tw	ClariNet UPI technology-related news.
clari.feature.dave_barry	Columns of humorist Dave Barry. (Moderated)
clari.feature.mike_royko	Chicago opinion columnist Mike Royko. (Moderated)
clari.biz.urgent	Breaking business news. (Moderated)
clari.news.law.crime	Major crimes. (Moderated)
clari.news.top	Top U.S. news stories. (Moderated)
clari.news.tv	TV schedules, news, reviews, and stars. (Moderated)
clari.news.urgent	Major breaking stories of the day. (Moderated)
clari.news.weather	Weather and temperature reports. (Moderated)
clari.sports.top	Top sports news. (Moderated)

gnu

gnUSENET is a set of newsgroups dealing with the GNU Project of the Free Software Foundation. GNU (GNU is not UNIX) will be a complete operating system, including application programs, with freely redistributable source code. These groups are also available as Internet mailing lists, and postings to Usenet or the Internet groups are "gatewayed" between the two systems. Questions about GNU can be directed to gnu@prep.ai.mit.edu.

pubnet

The pubnet hierarchy is designed for public-access UNIX systems (these systems are discussed at the end of Chapter Two). Current groups include:

pubnet.config	Pubnet connectivity discussions.
pubnet.nixpub	The "nixpub" list of public access UNIXes.
pubnet.sources	Software of interest to bbs users and sysops.
pubnet.talk	Miscellaneous bbs talk.
pubnet.test	Pubnet subnet testing.
pubnet.wanted	"Wanted" messages with a limited audience.
pubnet.sysops	Discussions between sysops of bbs systems.

Inet/DDN

Another alternative hierarchy of newsgroups is "Inet/DDN". This distribution consists of many newsgroups bearing names similar to traditional Usenet groups and corresponding to Internet discussion lists. Further details may be obtained by writing to Erik Fair (fair@ucbarpa.berkeley.edu).

Mailing List Etiquette

All of the etiquette tips mentioned in the "Electronic Mail Etiquette" section are applicable to mailing lists as well. However, there are some tips that are specifically for the mailing list environment.

The following list of tips was adapted from "A Primer on How to Work With the USENET Community," by Chuq Von Rospach. Although the original list was compiled for Usenet newsgroup communications, most of the tips have relevance to all mailing lists.

- **Strongly worded, emotional or angry responses are called "flaming," and are to be discouraged.**
  Don't respond to a message that angers you without giving yourself some time to think about how your response will be received. If you still want to send it, consider sending it via e-mail, rather than involving the entire mailing list in a "flame war." If you do decide to send the message to the list, be sure to warn readers that the comments might be perceived as inflammatory.

- **Don't blame system administrators for their users' or systems' behavior.**
  At times a mailer program may malfunction, resulting in a stream of duplicate or unrelated messages to list participants. Or a user from a particular system will post a series of inappropriate messages. If you believe that contacting a system administrator (or list moderator) is necessary, do so via e-mail, not over the mailing list. And don't assume that the administrator is aware of the problem; you may be the first to bring it to their attention.

- **Be careful what you say about others.**
  You never know who might be reading your messages. Mailing lists can have a very wide distribution. If you make a negative comment publicly about another person, it's entirely possible that the other person, his or her friends, or even your next employer, will see that message; this can end up reflecting even more negatively on you.

- **Be brief.**
  Many people pay by the minute for their access to the networks; the more concisely you state your message, the more likely it is to be read. This also means that you shouldn't quote any more from another message than is necessary to get your point across, and that if you use a "signature file," showing your name and address, that it should be brief as well.

- **Use descriptive titles.**
  If your title clearly shows the topic of your message, readers who are not directly interested in that topic can skip to the next message. This is important for the same reasons that brevity is important.

- **Think about your audience.**
  Send your messages to mailing lists or newsgroups that are specifically related to your message topic. If more than one group might be interested, don't automatically "cross-post" the message to all those groups. Many people subscribe to multiple groups, and will receive your message many times over.

- **Use mail to follow-up on messages whenever possible.**
  Often, mailing lists are used to post a query to a large group. It is often not necessary to send an answer to that same query to the same group. Instead, if you have an answer, send it to the person who posted the question via e-mail. If the topic is of general interest, that person can then summarize the responses received, and send that summary to the larger group. This helps eliminate message duplication.

- **Read all follow-ups and don't repeat what has already been said.**
  If you know the answer to a question, it's likely someone else does, as well. Check to see if the question has already been answered before you post a public response.

- **Be careful about copyrights and licenses.**
  The network provides a very large distribution medium. It should not be used for the distribution of copyrighted material. This includes reproduction of articles and other text, as well as distribution of copyrighted software.

- **Check your mailbox frequently.**
  If you don't, mail can pile up, and overload your mailbox. Reading (and deleting) messages regularly will save you from having to plow through piles of messages, and will keep you from abusing your system resources.

FTP

There have been many references in the preceding chapters to file transfer protocol (FTP). However, FTP is most often used to refer to the process of—rather than the protocol for—retrieving files from another computer on the Internet.

The FTP process involves the transfer of a file from one Internet host to another. Users with Phase One or Phase Two connectivity to the network will need a two-step process to retrieve files. First, the file must be transferred to their local host using an FTP server or an FTP program on the host computer. Next, the file must be transferred from the host computer to the desktop computer using a file transfer protocol like Kermit or Xmodem. Only users with Phase Three connectivity can use FTP to transfer a file directly to their desktop computer.

FTP has become the primary method of distribution for a large number of network-related files. The author of document can post it at one or more archives, and make it available to all network users. This allows the author to update the document easily at a central location, and removes the burden of distribution costs. Once the document has been added to an archive, the author will often send a message to related mailing lists announcing its location, so that interested mailing list participants will know how to retrieve the file.

A site is said to allow "anonymous FTP" when it permits users without accounts on its computer to retrieve files. For example, because the file server at the Coalition for Networked Information (ftp.cni.org) allows any network user to retrieve files, not just those with accounts on the cni.org computer, it is said to support anonymous FTP.

In the past, users needed to find FTP sites themselves, through referrals or printed lists. It was often a frustrating and time-consuming process to locate a site where a particular file could be found. Now, however, an application known as "Archie" helps users find the location for specific files quickly and easily. We describe the Archie program later in the chapter in the section on "Advanced Applications."

Phase One FTP: Using Gateways and FTP Servers

Only computers directly connected to the Internet can use FTP applications. However, users on networks with gateways to the Internet (Phase One connectivity) can retrieve some files via "FTP servers" which receive requests and send files via electronic mail. Two of these services are described below.

BITFTP

The BITFTP service at Princeton allows BITNET users who are not connected directly to the Internet to retrieve files from a variety of FTP sites.

BITFTP receives FTP commands via e-mail sent to BITFTP@PUCC (or to BITFTP@PUCC.Princeton.edu).

Send BITFTP a mail message containing only the text "FTPLIST" to receive a list of Internet hosts allowing anonymous FTP (not all hosts can necessarily be accessed via BITFTP). Send a message containing the text "HELP" to request a help file. A message with the text "VMS" will retrieve a collection of tips for users on VMS systems on retrieving binary files via BITFTP.

An FTP request should consist of a message with the following lines:

```
FTP hostname NETDATA (or: FTP hostname UUENCODE)
USER ANONYMOUS
<other ftp subcommands>
QUIT
```

Following the hostname on the FTP command, you may specify "UUENCODE" or NETDATA to tell BITFTP the format in which you wish to receive files. Most BITNET users should select "NETDATA" format. Those using BITFTP from a computer system using UUCP protocols may need to use the UUENCODE format.

The FTP subcommands include changing directories, doing directory listings, changing file mode and file types, and the actual retrieval of files. (these aspects of FTP are described in more detail in the sections below on Phase Two FTP service.

The following is an annotated example of a BITFTP FTP request:

```
FTP f.ms.uky.edu NETDATA
```

specifies the University of Kentucky host, and NETDATA format for retrieval of the file.

```
USER anonymous
```

logs you in as an anonymous user of the system.

```
CD /pub/msdos/Games
```

changes directories to the Games subdirectory.

```
DIR
```

does a directory listing of the current subdirectory (Games).

```
BINARY
```

changes file type to binary to allow the transfer of a software or compressed file, rather than a text file.

```
GET robotron.arc msdos.robotron
```

retrieves the file robotron.arc from the host system, and specifies that the copy received have the name "msdos.robotron".

```
QUIT
```

ends the FTP session.

The lines would all appear in a single e-mail message to the BITFTP server (without the annotations).

FTPMail

The Princeton BITFTP server was originally available to all network users, but the large number of requests it received made it necessary for the system administrators to limit it to BITNET users. In response, Paul Vixie of DEC set up an "FTPMail" system on one of DEC's computers.

To receive detailed information on using FTPMail, send an e-mail message to ftpmail@decwr.dec.com, with the word "HELP" in the body of the message. (No subject line is necessary.)

Some commands used by FTPMail are described below.

```
connect [HOST [USER [PASS]]]
```

connects to a specific FTP site. The default is FTPMail's home site, gatekeeper.dec.com, as an anonymous user.

```
ascii
```

specifies ASCII file type for text files.

```
binary
```

specifies binary file type for compressed, formatted, or software files.

```
chdir
```

changes directories. Only one CHDIR can be used in any one FTPMail request.

```
ls (or dir)
```

provides a brief directory listing of file names; the dir command provides a longer listing with file sizes.

```
get FILE filename
```

specifies a file to be mailed to you. Up to ten GET commands can be used in a single FTPMail session.

```
quit
```

ends the FTPMail session. Any lines following this in the message will be ignored.

A sample FTPMail message, retrieving the file "00README" from the /pub/software directory of the ftp.cni.org server, is shown below:

```
To: ftpmail@decwrl.dec.com
Subject:

connect ftp.cni.org
chdir /pub/software
ascii
get 00README
quit
```

Phase Two FTP: Using Host Applications

The majority of Internet users will use a host application to retrieve files via FTP. Although application interfaces will vary from one machine to another, the basic steps involved are fairly standard on all systems. A representative session is shown below, with annotations.

1. Establish a connection to the host machine. You can use either the host name, or the numeric Internet Protocol (IP) address. The name is generally better, as IP addresses can sometimes change. However, not all systems will allow users to specify the host by name, so the IP address may be necessary.

```
a.cni.org> ftp ftp.cni.org  or ftp xxx.xxx.xxx
Connected to a.cni.org.
220 a.cni.org FTP server (Ultrix Version 4.1 Mon Aug 27 19:11:56
EDT 1990) read.
```

2. Login as an anonymous user. (When a site supports anonymous FTP, that means that any user can connect with a user name of "anonymous.")

```
Name (ftp.cni.org:llane): anonymous
331 Guest login ok, send ident as password.
```

3. Send your e-mail address as a password. Some systems will prompt you to send "ident," which means your identity. Others will explicitly ask for your id and address. Although the system will not refuse you access if you do not provide this information, it is considered a courtesy to the system administrator, who may be tracking usage from different sites.

```
Password: yourid@your.address
230 Guest login ok, access restrictions apply.
```

4. List the contents of the directory to see what files and directories are available.

```
ftp> dir
200 PORT command successful.
150 Opening data connection for
/bin/ls (192.100.21.1,2289) (0 bytes).
total 7
drwxr-xr-x   11   0   0   512   Apr 22   13:47   CNI
drwxr-xr-x    2   0   0   512   Feb 6    18:28   bin
drwxr-xr-x    2   0   0   512   Apr 22   13:48   current.cites
drwxr-xr-x    2   0   0   512   Feb 6    17:18   etc
d-x-x-x       4   0   0   512   Mar 31   17:33   incoming
d-x-x-x       3   0   0   512   May 9    17:18   members
drwxr-xr-x    6   0   0   512   Mar 31   17:45   pub
226 Transfers complete.
441 bytes received in 0.25 seconds (1.7 Kbytes/s)
```

5. If necessary, change to a different directory. Many systems maintain a "pub" directory, in which they place files meant for public distribution. This is always a good place to begin looking for information.

```
ftp> cd pub
250 CWD command successful.

ftp> dir
200 PORT command successful.
150 Opening data connection for /bin/ls
(192.100.21.1,2292) (0 bytes).
total 4
drwxr-xr-x    2    0    0    512    May 20    13:11    FYI-RFC
drwxr-xr-x    2    0    0    512    Apr 1     01:21    MARBI
drwxr-xr-x    3    0    0    512    Apr 1     00:36    arl.directory
drwxr-xr-x   10    0    0    512    Apr 13    18:24    software

ftp> cd software
250 CWD command successful.

ftp> dir
200 PORT command successful.
150 Opening data connection for /bin/ls
(192.100.21.1,2294) (0 bytes).
total 9
-rw-r—r—     1    0    0      2    Mar 23    11:18    00README
drwxr-xr-x    2    0    0    512    Mar 23    12:26    BinHex
drwxr-xr-x    2    0    0    512    Mar 23    11:42    brown.tn3270
drwxr-xr-x    2    0    0    512    Mar 23    21:10    byu.Telnet
drwxr-xr-x    2    0    0    512    Apr 7     14:31    hyperftp
drwxr-xr-x    2    0    0    512    Apr 13    18:24    hyTelnet
drwxr-xr-x    6    0    0    512    Mar 23    14:17    internet.gopher
drwxr-xr-x    2    0    0    512    Mar 23    13:03    mud.dweller
drwxr-xr-x    2    0    0    512    Mar 23    21:05    ncsa.Telnet
226 Transfers complete.
602 bytes received in 0.25 seconds (2.3 Kbytes/s)
```

6. If the directory has a README or an INDEX file, retrieve it first; it will provide more information on the site.

   If you are retrieving a text file, and are not sure if the default mode on your system is for text, set the mode to ASCII. If you are retrieving a binary (application, formatted, or compressed) file, set the mode to Binary.

```
ftp> ascii
200 Representation type is now ASCII Nonprint.
```

7. Retrieve the file using the GET command. The first name specified is the filename as it appears on the host site. If you do not specify a second name, the file will be retrieved with the same name on your home system. However, because not all systems have the same file naming conventions, it is often helpful to rename the file. Also, since you may retrieve a number of files with the name README or INDEX, you should rename them when retrieving them to avoid confusion.

```
ftp> get 00README readme.cni
200 PORT command successful.
150 Opening data connection for 00README
(192.100.21.1,2296) (2 bytes).
226 Transfer complete.
local: readme.cni remote: 00README
4 bytes received in 0.0039 seconds (1 Kbytes/s)
```

8. When you are done retrieving files, exit from the FTP session with the QUIT command.

```
ftp> quit
221 Goodbye.
```

Directory names are often self-explanatory, often having names like "software," "maps," or "guides." Some directory names are standard on many systems, like "pubs" for descriptive publication files.

Another useful command is ls, which will provide a brief list of directory contents. The ls -CF command will show the listing by screen, and ls -l will provide a more detailed list of the directory, including file size, and differentiating between subdirectories and files.

Phase Three FTP: Using Desktop Applications

Users with direct desktop connectivity often have more flexibility and power in their FTP programs. Many of the commands that must be remembered and entered by Phase One and Phase Two users are handled by the software for Phase Three users.

Currently, many of the desktop applications available for FTP are designed for use on Macintosh systems. The Mac's graphical user interface and multitasking are well-suited these applications. As more workstations become connected to the Internet, more of these applications, for a wider range of operating systems, will become available.

Two relatively new programs for desktop FTP are described below.

HyperFTP

HyperFTP is a HyperCard stack that can be used on any Macintosh running HyperCard 1.3 or higher, and using the MacTCP driver to connect to the Internet. It allows users to preview text files on the FTP host site before downloading, and can perform BinHex decompression while retrieving Macintosh files in ".hqx" format (more information on BinHex is provided in Chapter Three).

HyperFTP was written by Douglas Hornig (DUG@CornellC.CIT.Cornell.edu) and is public domain software; it is distributed free of charge, but may not be resold.

The HyperFTP stack is available from the ftp.cni.org host, in the /pub/software/hyperftp subdirectory.

XferIt

XferIt is a stand-alone application that allows Macintosh users running MacTCP to transfer files to and from FTP archives. XferIt's interface represents folders and files as multiple windows. Simultaneous connections to multiple transfer hosts are permitted, all with a consistent interface. The program recognizes VAX/VMS, UNIX, VM/CMS, and Macintosh FTP servers, and supports several different transfer modes, including text, binary, MacBinary, and BinHex. XferIt is shareware, and a single user license is available for a payment of $10.00.

The software is available on the ftp.cni.org host, in the /pub/software/xferit subdirectory.

TELNET

Telnet is an application that allows users to remotely log into one Internet host while connected to another. For example, a person with an account on two different university's computers could log into one system, and then use Telnet to log into the second system. No long-distance charges would apply, because the communication would be taking place over Internet wiring, rather than over commercial telephone lines.

A more common use of Telnet is to allow network users to remotely log into network resources like library catalogs and database servers. Many systems allow "guest" logins so as to allow access to information resources. (The LIBS, LIBTEL, and HytelNet programs described in Chapter Five all use Telnet software to make connections to remote library systems.)

Because Telnet is a "live" Internet activity, it can only be accomplished by Phase Two and Phase Three network users; a gateway connection, which provides batch services, cannot be used for remote logins.

Most new network users will use Telnet from Phase Two terminals connected to a host computer. On some computers, it is necessary to enter a command (or series of commands) to make the Telent software available. If you try typing "telnet" at your system prompt and get an error message in response, check with your computing center for more information on using the Telnet package.

Standard Telnet

When using Telnet to connect to a host computer that is *not* an IBM mainframe, you will generally type the command "telnet" followed by the name or IP address of the host to which you wish to connect.

An example of a Telnet command appears below:

```
prompt> telnet 255.255.255.255 or telnet host.zone.domain.class
Trying...
Connected to 255.255.255.255.
Escape character is '^ '.
```

After the Telnet program connects to the specified host, that computer's login screen will appear. If you have an account on the host computer, you log into that host as you would with a direct connection. If you are connecting to a computer that has resources available to non-affiliated users (such as a public access computer catalog, or campus-wide information system), you will need to follow instructions for that local system. Guest login procedures vary greatly from one site to another. Some of the guides described in Chapter Five provide information on the specific login procedures for available Telnet sites.

```
ULTRIX V4.1 (Rev. 52) (host.zone.domain.class)

login: userid
password: password will not appear when typed in

<<login message here>>

prompt>
```

After you enter the correct login information, you will be logged into the host computer system, and can use the resources available on that system as if you were logged in at a local terminal.

Telnet and IBM Mainframes

When connecting to an IBM mainframe system from a non-IBM host computer, it is often necessary to use a variation of the Telnet software called "tn3270." This Telnet package allows you to emulate an IBM 3270 terminal when connecting to an IBM host system.

To the end-user, tn3270 software works much like standard telnet software. The only difference is that the command "tn3270" is used instead of "Telnet."

When your home system is an IBM mainframe, you may have difficulty in using Telnet to connect to non-IBM hosts. If you attempt to telnet to another system from an IBM host and find that your screen displays are garbled and filled with nonsensical characters ("control characters"), this is a function of your host system's inability to "talk" with non-IBM systems. Some IBM mainframes provide a feature known as "transparent mode," which allows trouble-free connections to non-IBM systems. Without this feature, the IBM defaults to "line mode," which is incapable of properly translating the VT100 terminal control characters sent by the other computer.

Finger

The finger command is available on many Internet hosts. It allows you to find information about a user on a given system, if you know their full address.

To use the command, enter:

```
finger keyword@hostname.domain
```

For example, to find Craig Summerhill at the Coalition for Networked Information (a.cni.org), you would enter the following command:

```
a.cni.org> finger craig@a.cni.org
```

or the last name:

```
a.cni.org> finger summerhill@a.cni.org
```

Your query would yield the following result:

```
[a.cni.org]
Login name: craig              In real life: Craig A. Summerhill
Office: CNI, (202) 232-2466
Directory: /usr/users/craig        Shell: /bin/csh
Last login Sat May 2 13:40 on ttyp1 from annex.cni.org
Plan:

I am the Systems Coordinator at the Coalition for Networked In-
formation. Questions about any of the resources on this server
should be directed to me.

snailnet:      1527 New Hampshire Ave., N.W.
               Washington, D.C.  20036

Internet:      craig@cni.org
at&tnet:       (202) 232-2466
faxnet:        (202) 462-7849
icbmnet:       ??
```

The amount of information you receive with a finger command will depend on the system you are querying, and the individual user. Some systems, for security reasons, do not allow information to be obtained via the finger command. Even on systems that do allow access, the information provided may be minimal, showing only the login and real names, and last login.

When the finger application is executed without a login ID or address as an argument, the application will generally return a list of users currently logged onto the local host. The display shown below was generated by a finger application running on an Ultrix operating system.

```
a.cni.org> finger
Login     Name      TTY   Idle   When         Office
john      John Doe  p0           Mon 18:06    3065
jane      Jane Doe  p2    12      Mon 15:32    2201
```

A list of users logged onto a specific host on the network can be returned using the finger application with an @address as an argument.

```
a.cni.org> finger @address
finger @host.domain
[host.domain]
Friday, Apr 10, 1992 5:49PM-CDT  Up 3 06:53:27
24+1 Jobs  Load ave 0.69 0.65 0.64
User     Personal Name  Job       Subsys  Idle   TTY    Console Location
USER     Doe, John Q.   20C00B71  *DCL*          nty3   TCP:host.domain
USER2    Doe, Jane      20C00C4E  TELNET  11.    nty2   lta6133LAT:
```

More information on the technical aspects of the finger protocol is provided in Chapter Three.

Advanced Applications

The applications described above are considered "basic" Internet applications, in that they provide a straightforward service to users that can be implemented on almost any Internet host. These applications are governed by network standards, and are the basis for the bulk of network communications.

Over the past several years, however, a number of innovative applications have been developed for use on the Internet. These applications provide users with a variety of additional capabilities. However, in order to take advantage of these capabilities, users often need advanced workstations, as well. Although most of the applications below were designed for users with Phase Three connectivity, pared-down versions of the client software have been developed for some, allowing them to be run by users with Phase Two connectivity.

Client/Server Model

The applications we describe below are based on a "client-server" model of processing. These applications have two basic parts: a "server," which stores the raw data that will be used, and the "client," which provides a user-friendly interface to the server's data. The primary advantage of client-server computing is that the server and its data can be located on a single network computer, eliminating the need to maintain duplicate copies of the data. Users on any Internet host can then access the data on the server, using a front-end interface that can be customized for their local computer.

Some specific implementations of client/server software applications on the Internet are described below.

Archie

Although FTP provides Internet users with access to thousands of files across the network, the large number of FTP archive sites on the Internet often makes it difficult for users to find the right site for a specific file. The McGill University School of Computer Science has developed a tool they call "Archie" to address this problem.

Archie consists of a pair of software tools: the server software, which maintains a regularly updated list of over 600 archive sites and files, and the user software, which allows users to search the Archie database.

The Archie server software does a nightly scan of a subset of the archive site list, and retrieves a directory listing from each. The information is then stored in the Archie database. Approximately one thirtieth of the total list is scanned each night, which means that every site is updated about once a month.

Network users can Telnet to an Archie site, and search the database for specific software. Because Archie provides one central database for all the archive sites the Archie system managers know of, it greatly speeds the task of finding a specific program on the network.

System managers can install Archie client software on their local systems, which allows users to query the database remotely. With this capability, a user can enter a single command line query, and have the results sent to a file on the local system.

To access Archie at the McGill site, you can Telnet to quiche.cs.mcgill.ca (132.206.2.3), and login with the user name "archie."

Once connected to the Archie site (or running Archie client software on your local system), you will see an "archie" prompt. At that prompt, you can enter your query. .

An annotated Archie session is shown below. In this example, the query is for a program called Retrospect:

```
archie> prog Retrospect
# matches / % database searched:      0 / 0%    0 / 4%
    0 / 8%       0 / 12%      0 / 16%   0 / 20%   0 / 24%
    0 / 28%      0 / 32%      2 /       4 /       4 / 36%
    4 / 40%      4 / 44%      4 / 48%   4 / 52%   4 / 56%
    4 / 60%      4 / 64%      4 / 68%   5 /       5 / 72%
    5 / 76%      5 / 80%      5 / 84%   5 / 88%   5 / 92%
    5 / 96%
Host rascal.ics.utexas.edu   (128.83.138.20)
Last updated 02:33 8 Jan 1992
```

The numbers appearing below the query are indications of the Archie program's progress as it searches through the archives. The number before the slash shows the number of occurrences of the program name in the archives, and the number after the slash shows the percentage of the available archives searched.

The Archie program then displays the location and name of each of the occurrences it found.

```
Location: /misc/mac/system-related
   FILE   rw-rw-r— 363    Apr 16 1989   Retrospect_DEMO_intro
Host gate.oxy.edu  (134.69.1.2)
Last updated 15:11 31 Dec 1991


Location: /public/Mac_Programs
   FILE   rw-r—r— 36     Mar 27 1991   Retrospect_DEMO_intro

Host rascal.ics.utexas.edu  (128.83.138.20)
Last updated 02:33 8 Jan 1992


Location: /misc/mac/system-related
   FILE   rw-rw-r— 105216 Apr 16 1989   Retrospect_DEMO_stack_sit_bin

Host gate.oxy.edu  (134.69.1.2)
Last updated 15:11 31 Dec 1991


Location: /public/Mac_Programs
   FILE   rw-r—r— 105216 Mar 27 1991   Retrospect_DEMO_stack_sit_bin

Host rascal.ics.utexas.edu  (128.83.138.20)
Last updated 02:33 8 Jan 1992


Location:/misc/mac/comp.sys.mac.announce/+_miscellaneous
   FILE   rw-rw-r— 2832   Oct 31 08:07 Retrospect-
                                       Remote_server_problem


     archie>
```

Some other archie server sites are:

> archie.sura.net (SURAnet)
> archie.unl.edu (University of Nebraska in Lincoln)
> archie.ans.net (ANS archie server)
> quiche.cs.mcgill.ca (Canada server, original archie site)
> archie.au (Australian server)
> archie.funet.fi (European server in Finland)
> archie.doc.ic.ac.uk (UK/England server)

WAIS

Wide Area Information Server (WAIS, pronounced "ways") is a set of programs (and a protocol) that allow users to search and access different types of information from a single interface. This information can be in any format (e.g., text, sound, images), and can reside anywhere on the network. The WAIS protocol is an extension of the ANSI Z39.50 information retrieval protocol, which is described in more detail in Chapter Three.

WAIS client software has been written for a variety of computer systems. The most elegant implementations are designed for use on workstations with Phase Three connectivity; these programs are available for Macintosh, NeXT, and X Windows operating systems. WAIS clients are also available for use on GNU Emacs, and UNIX shell environments. A command-line interface for use on "dumb terminals" (Phase Two connectivity) is in beta-testing as of this writing.

The WAIS client allows the user to specify one or more sources of information (servers), and to formulate a query for those sources. Current WAIS implementations use a string of keywords for the query; however, because WAIS is actually a protocol rather than a specific program, future implementations could use more complex query formulations. (In fact, the 1992 version of the Z39.50 protocol allows for the use of Boolean logic, which may well be incorporated in future releases of WAIS software.)

Thinking Machines, the company that originated the WAIS concept, maintains a WAIS server, directory-of-servers.src, which is a "white pages" of other WAIS servers. You can query this WAIS server to find other servers and new ones that become available. When a new WAIS server is made available, the individual or organization maintaining that server can register it with the directory-of-servers.

More detailed information on WAIS, as well as client software for several operating environments, is available via anonymous FTP from the site think.com, in the subdirectory /public/wais. The filename for WAIS version 8 beta 3.1 is: wais-8-b3.1.tar.Z; and, for the Mac client/interface: WAIStation-0-62.sit.hqx. A bibliography of WAIS-related articles is available via anonymous ftp from quake.think.com, as /pub/wais/wais-discussion/bibliography.txt.

There are also three mailing lists related to WAIS, all of which are maintained at think.com:

1. The wais-interest@think.com group provides announcements of new releases for the Internet environment. Approximately one message per month. To join, send mail to wais-interest-request@think.com.
2. The wais-discussion@think.com group is a moderated digest of mail from users and developers on electronic publishing and other WAIS-related topics. It includes all messages from wais-interest. To join, send mail to wais-discussion-request@think.com.
3. The wais-talk@think.com is an unmoderated list for implementors and interactive discussions. To join, send mail to wais-talk-request@think.com.

Internet Gopher

Internet Gopher is a distributed document delivery service. It allows even novice network users to seamlessly access data residing on multiple hosts. The client program presents the user with a hierarchical arrangement of documents.

Internet Gopher servers accept simple queries (sent over an Internet connection), and respond by sending the client a document or a list of documents. The client-server design allows multiple servers to respond transparently to the user client's request

Gopher clients are available from the University of Minnesota for Mac, IBM-PC compatible, IBM VM/CMS, and UNIX based systems. The University of St. Thomas has a NeXT gopher client available for anonymous FTP from cs.stthomas.edu (140.209.5.1). (The client software for desktop machines requires Phase Three connectivity.)

More information about the Gopher protocol is available via anonymous FTP from boombox.micro.umn.edu, in the /pub/gopher directory. You can subscribe to a mailing list for announcements of new gopher servers and software by sending a request to gopher-news-request@boombox.micro.umn.edu.

The gopher system can be accessed via Telnet sessions to the University of Minnesota, at consultant.micro.umn.edu (login as "gopher").

Chapter Five: Network Resources

This chapter describes two types of network resources: those that assist users in navigating through the Internet, and those that provide primary source material for research and entertainment. The resources described below are only a small sample of the many resources available over the Internet. New materials become available on a daily basis. However, we have tried to provide enough information for you to get a taste of the riches available over the networks.

Internet Resource Guide

The National Science Foundation (NSF) Network Service Center (NNSC) publishes a guide to resources on the Internet. These resources include facilities such as supercomputers, databases, libraries, or specialized programs on the Internet which are available to large numbers of users. Each entry in the Internet Resource Guide contains a description of the resource, a description of who may use the resource, the type of access supported (e-mail, FTP, Telnet), and contact points for further information such as a phone number, e-mail address, and name of a contact person where appropriate. Each listing is approximately one page of text.

The guide may be retrieved via anonymous FTP from nnsc.nsf.net, in the directory resource-guide. It can also be browsed online via the CARL online library system.

For more information on the Internet Resource Guide, the e-mail address is nnsc@nnsc.nsf.net.

Internet Tour HyperCard Stack

The NNSC has released a HyperCard 2™ stack entitled "Tour of the Internet." The tour is designed as a general introduction to the Internet and includes information on the history of the Internet, network etiquette, and network applications as well as a glossary of networking terms. It is designed for the new network user.

The tour is available for anonymous FTP on nnsc.nsf.net, in the directory internet-tour. The filename is Internet-Tour.sit.hqx.

For more information on the tour, contact the NNSC at nnsc@nnsc.nsf.net, or (617) 873-3400.

The Internet Explorer's Toolkit

"The Internet Explorer's Toolkit" is a hypertext system for MS-DOS based computers, created by Ernest Perez. Designed for professional librarians, it is a basic toolkit for getting up to speed fast in network skills and specialized knowledge. It contains a collection of useful text files about using the Internet, as well as a copy of PSILink—a shareware program and commercial online service providing dialup access to the Internet. (PSILink is described in more detail in Chapter Two.)

The full toolkit consists of two zipped (compressed) files: 1) EXPLORER.ZIP and 2) PSILINK.ZIP.

EXPLORER.ZIP contains a hypertext runtime program and the full-text contents of the system. It runs completely independently of the second zipped file. It is approximately 245K in size.

PSILINK.ZIP contains a compressed version of the shareware copyrighted PSILink program, distributed by Performance Systems International, Inc. This program allows users to direct dial into the Internet by local call in over 150 U.S. cities. PSILink service is a commercial service, priced at levels with different grades of service and modem speed levels. Information about the service, telephone numbers, and installation instructions for the shareware program are included in the EXPLORER.ZIP hypertext system.

More information on the Explorer's Toolkit is available from:

Ernest Perez, Ph.D
Access Information Associates
2183 Buckingham, Suite 106
Richardson TX 75081
(214) 530-4800
Internet: eperez@utdallas.edu
BITNET: eperez@utdallas

Merit Internet Cruise

The Merit Network, Inc., which oversees the operations of the NSFnet backbone, has created the Merit Internet Cruise, a Macintosh-based instructional guide to the Internet. It requires: a Macintosh II or Quadra with color monitor and FDHD disk drive; system 6.07 or higher; approximately 2MB of available disk space; and 4MB RAM.

The introduction section of the guide compares the Internet to an ocean. In the navigation tools section, there are descriptions of some Internet tools, including e-mail, FTP, and Telnet. The applications section includes several examples of how people are using some of the Internet resources and how to access those resources.

The Merit Internet Cruise is available via FTP from the Merit archives, at nic.merit.edu. To retrieve the program:

1. Use anonymous FTP to connect to nic.merit.edu, change directories to internet/resources, and get the file "merit.cruise.sea.hqx". Because the file has been converted to BinHex format (see Chapter Three for more information on BinHex), it can be retrieved as a text file.
2. Convert this file using BinHex 4.0. (The Macintosh compression programs StuffIt and Compact Pro also have options to "unbinhex" a file.)

3. Double click on the file "Merit's Cruise.sea" to begin the extraction process.
4. When prompted, select your destination volume (it should have at least 2MB of disk space available).
5. With the destination drive selected, click on the Extract button. The file "Merit's Cruise" will automatically be extracted and copied to your selected hard drive.
6. To run the Cruise, double click on your copy of the file "Merit's Cruise."

The beta version (1.0.Beta) of Merit Network's "Cruise of the Internet" is being distributed without charge for evaluation and use. Merit is interested in what you think of this presentation and how you might want to use it. Send your comments via e-mail to cruise-feedback@merit.edu.

User input will be considered during the development of the next version. Version 2.0, when ready, will also be available via anonymous FTP on nic.merit.edu in the internet/resources directory. A DOS-Windows version may be available at that time.

Zen and the Art of the Internet

Zen and the Art of the Internet is an introductory guide to using the Internet written by Brendan Kehoe. The guide addresses topics such as electronic mail, Telnet and FTP, domain names, and a variety of other topics. A glossary and bibliography are also included.

The guide is directed toward individuals who currently have Internet access via a host computer, and need straightforward, non-system-specific instructions on how to use the resources available to them. Although Kehoe does not limit the guide to a single operating system environment, it has a slight bias toward the UNIX operating system.

The guide was originally distributed only via the networks, and was not available in printed form. Kehoe is now publishing the book commercially, and it should be available in late 1992 or early 1993.

The original guide will continue to be available via anonymous FTP from a number of sites. It is stored in three formats: a .tar.Z file, for UNIX system users; a .dvi file (output from TeX typesetting system); and a .PS (Postscript) file. All of these files require specific printers or software for output. There are plans to release the guide in ASCII text form as an FYI RFC (see the description of these files later in this chapter) some time in 1992.

The most recent versions of the files are available from the following FTP archive sites:

- ftp.uu.net [137.39.1.9] in /inet/doc
- ftp.cs.toronto.edu [128.100.3.6] in pub/zen
- ftp.cs.widener.edu [147.31.254.132] in pub/zen as zen-1.0.tar.Z, zen-1.0.dvi, and zen-1.0.PS
- ftp.sura.net [128.167.254.179] in pub/nic as zen-1.0.PS

Yanoff's Special Internet Connections List

One of the most valuable lists of primary source materials on the Internet is the Special Internet Connections list maintained by Scott Yanoff of the University of Wisconsin. This list, which is updated on a bi-weekly basis, includes over one hundred valuable references to sources of information on the Internet, including up-to-date baseball scores, top 40 charts, weather maps, Internet Gopher and Archie servers, and information databases.

The file is available via anonymous FTP from the csd.uwm.edu site. The file, called internet.services.txt, is in the pub directory.

UNIX system users can get updated information on the guide by fingering yanoff@csd4.csd.uwm.edu.

Crossing the Internet Threshold

Crossing the Internet Threshold, by Roy Tennant, John Ober, and Anne G. Lipow, is a revised edition of the workbook that supported June 1992 workshops of the same name. It is addressed to two categories of reader: the person who has access to the Internet and wants to learn how to take advantage of its vast resources, and the person who wants to teach Internet skills to others.

The book includes exercises in e-mail, Telnet, and FTP (for beginners and advanced learners); a glossary and "fact sheets" (single-page summaries of major network systems and services, from Archie to Z39.50); sample overheads (for trainers); and network maps.

For more information, write to:

Address: Library Solutions Institute and Press
          1100 Indsutrial Rd, Suite 9
          San Carlos, CA 94070
Phone: (510) 841-2636
Fax: (510) 841-2926

NorthWestNet User Services Internet Resource Guide

The user services staff of the NorthWestNet network has produced a comprehensive guide to using the Internet for their users. The guide, NYSIRG, is also applicable to users on other Internet hosts, and NorthWestNet is now distributing electronic copies of the guide via anonymous FTP, and selling printed copies upon request.

This extensive (over 300 pages) guide covers a range of topics, including: the role of the network service provider (in this case, NorthWestNet); basic tools such as e-mail, FTP, and Telnet; mailing lists; online resources; K-12 networking; and scientific research on the networks.

The FTP site for the files is ftphost.nwnet.net. The files are located in the nic/nwnet/user-guide directory, with the following filenames:

Filenames	Brief Description of Contents
README.nusirg	Introductory information
nusirg.Index.ps	Index for all of NUSIRG
nusirg.about.nwnet.and.aup.ps	Information about NWNET and NSFnet
nusirg.beginner.overview.ps	Overview of NUSIRG and the Internet
nusirg.email.ftp.Telnet.ps	E-mall, FTP, TELNET and Archie
nusirg.listserv.usenet.ps	USENET and LISTSERV
nusirg.online.info.resources.ps	Electronic books, electronic journals, online library catalogs, databases and bibliographies, WAIS, and Internet directories
nusirg.supercomputers.ps	Supercomputers on the Internet
nusirg.teach.k-12.ps	The Internet and K-12 education
nusirg.whole-guide.ps.Z	All of NUSIRG in compressed format

There are several things to keep in mind before retrieving any of these files:

- Files with .ps filename extensions are in PostScript format, and can be printed only on PostScript printers. An ASCII text version is being prepared as well, and will be available in the same with .txt filename extensions when it is complete.
- The file "nusirg.whole-guide.ps.Z" is not an archive, but is a 450KB compressed version of the entire 300-page document; uncompressed, this file is about 1.4MB in size. Be certain you have enough room on your host machine before you attempt to retrieve and uncompress this file.
- Before printing "nusirg.whole-guide.ps.Z", you must decompress the file with software appropriate to your computer's operating system. (Information on file compression software is provided in Chapter Three.)

Printed and bound copies of NUSIRG are available at $20 per copy (plus tax for Washington State residents), and may be ordered from:

```
Address:  NorthWestNet
          NUSIRG Orders
          15400 SE 30th Place, Suite 202
          Bellevue, WA 98007
E-mail:   nusirg-orders@nwnet.net
Phone:    (206) 562-3000
```

NYSERNet New User's Guide

NYSERNet, Inc.'s *New User's Guide to Useful and Unique Resources on the FTP* is available in a bound, paper version, or in ASCII format from their FTP server. The current version, version 2.2, contains information about fifty-two resources using Telnet, FTP, and electronic mail. The guide describes each service, provides step-by-step instructions to access the service, and gives the exit command (for Telnet sites).

The cost of the paper version of the guide is $18 for NYSERNet affiliates and interest group members, and $25 for non-affiliates. (Bulk discounts are available.)

The text version is available via anonymous FTP from the nysernet.org archives. The file is called "new.user.guide.v2.2.txt," and it is in the /pub/guides subdirectory.

The guide can also be browsed interactively via the NYSERView system, which can be reached by telneting to nysernet.org, and logging in as "nyserview" with a password of "nyserview".

NYSERView allows travel, via Telnet, to any of the resources featured in the guide. The system is menu-driven, and easy to use, designed primarily for the new or infrequent Internet user. Future plans will expand this resource for New York State.

For further information on this guide, or on the NYSERView service, contact:

    Address: NYSERNet, Inc.
              111 College Place - Room 3-211
              Syracuse, NY 13244-4100
    E-mail: info@nysernet.org
    Phone: (315) 443-4120
    Fax: (315) 425-7518

SURAnet Internet Resource Guide

The SURAnet Internet Resource Guide contains a wealth of information on resources accessible via the Internet. The SURAnet Internet Resource Guide is available for ftp from FTP.SURA.NET and is located in the pub/nic directory. This Guide is updated weekly and the sources are varified monthly. The name of the file is, infoguide.x-xx, where x-xx is the most current version.

For more information, contact the SURAnet Network Information Center at:

    Address: SURAnet
              8400 Baltimore Blvd.
              Suite 101
              College Park, MD 20740
    E-mail: suranet-admin@noc.sura.net

InfoPop

InfoPop, a hypertext guide to using the Internet, is available for IBM-compatible microcomputers in both TSR and stand-alone forms. The TSR version can be swapped out to disk or EMS when not active, so it uses only about 8K of RAM.

InfoPop allows users to cut and paste from the InfoPop hypertext search system to their underlying application (a terminal program, for example). This save users from having to remember Telnet addresses.

InfoPop provides a tutorial system on what various Internet resources offer and how to use them, and an address book for locating the resources. It includes information on the Internet, BITNET, CompuServe, dial-up bbs systems and more.

InfoPop is available free of charge from George Mason University's GMUtant OnLine bbs. (Dial 703-993-2219, using a 1200, 2400, or 9600 bps modem. The v.32 protocol is supported.) It can also be retrieved via FTP from FTP.UNT.EDU in the library directory.

NICs and NOCs

Network Information Centers (NICs) are organizations that provide network users with information about services provided by the network. Network Operations Centes (NOCs) are organizations responsible for maintaining a network.

Most NSFnet backbone networks and mid-level regional networks have both an NIC and an NOC. Smaller networks often combine the functions of the NIC and the NOC into a single organization.

The NICs at some of the major Internet sites have become primary distributors of information about their own networks and the Internet as a whole. In particular, the NICs at the Defense Data Network (nic.ddn.mil) and at the NSFnet Network Service Center (nnsc.nsf.net) have taken on responsibility for serving as distribution points for network Request for Comments (RFCs, described in the next section), network descriptions, and informational files and programs.

RFCs

Requests for Comments (RFCs) are working notes of the Internet research and development community. A document in this series may be on essentially any topic related to computer communications, and may be anything from a meeting report to the specification of a standard.

The majority of RFCs are geared toward the technical networking community: engineers, programmers, and other system "architects." They address network protocols and services, and provide detailed descriptions of procedures for implementing Internet technology.

The complete set of all RFCs issued is maintained at, and available from, the Defense Data Network (DDN) NIC at SRI International. For further information, contact the NIC by telephone at (800) 235-3155, or by electronic mail to NIC@NIC.DDN.MIL.

Subsets of this master set (shadow copies) are maintained at several NIC sites, including nnsc.nsf.net. Use of the RFC repositories at these sites may be more suitable to your network connectivity requirements. However, the NIC.DDN.MIL is the central repository and will contain the most up-to-date set of RFCs.

RFCs are available to network users through several FTP archives. The primary site is nic.ddn.mil, but many other network information centers, including nnsc.nsf.net, make these files available to users.

If you do not have FTP access, but do have electronic mail, there are several mail servers that can send an RFC to you directly.

The NSFnet Network Information Service (NIS) provides an automatic mail service for those sites that cannot use FTP. Address the request to NIS-INFO@NIS.NSF.NET and leave the subject field of the message blank. The first line of the text of the message must be "SEND RFC*nnnn*.TXT-1", where *nnnn* is the RFC number. This means that the format of the online files must meet the constraints of a wide variety of printing and display equipment.

JvNCnet also provides a mail service for those sites that cannot use FTP. Address the request to SENDRFC@JVNC.NET and in the subject field of the message indicate the RFC number, as in "Subject: RFC *nnnn*". For the latest RFC Index, simply type "index" in the subject line.

FYI RFCs

The FYI series of notes is designed to provide Internet users with a central repository of information about any topics related to the Internet. The FYIs are intended for a wide audience, and address issues of interest to both advanced and beginning readers. The topics of the FYI RFCs range from descriptions of Internet history and procedures to "Q & As" for new and experienced network users.

FYIs can be obtained via FTP from NIC.DDN.MIL, with the same procedure described in the section above on RFCs. They can be requested using the RFC number provided, or by using FYI:*mm*.TXT, where *mm* refers to the FYI number. To retrieve the files via e-mail from the FTP mail server at NIC.DDN.MIL, address the request to SERVICE@NIC.DDN.MIL and in the subject field of the message indicate the FYI or RFC number, as in "Subject: FYI *mm*" or "Subject: RFC *nnnn*".

The list of FYIs, as of April 1992, was as follows:

1. Malkin, G.S.; Reynolds, J.K. *F.Y.I. on F.Y.I.: Introduction to the F.Y.I. notes.* 1990 March; 4 p. (Format: TXT=7867 bytes) (Also RFC 1150)

2. Stine, R.H.,ed. *FYI on a network management tool catalog: Tools for monitoring and debugging TCP/IP internets and interconnected devices.* 1990 April; 126 p. (Format: TXT=336906 PS=555225 bytes) (Also RFC 1147)

3. Bowers, K.L.; LaQuey, T.L.; Reynolds, J.K.; Roubicek, K.; Stahl, M.K.; Yuan, A. *FYI on where to start: A bibliography of internetworking information.* 1990 August; 42 p. (Format: TXT=67330 bytes) (Also RFC 1175)

4. Malkin, G.S.; Marine, A.N. *FYI on Questions and Answers: Answers to commonly asked "new Internet user" questions.* 1991 February; 32 p. (Format: TXT=72479 bytes) (Also RFC 1206) (Obsoletes RFC 1177)

5. Libes, D. *Choosing a name for your computer.* 1990 August; 8 p. (Format: TXT=18472 bytes) (Also RFC 1178)

6. Scheifler, R.W. *FYI on the X window system.* 1991 January; 3 p. (Format: TXT=3629 bytes) (Also RFC 1198)

7. Malkin, G.S.; Marine, A.N.; Reynolds, J.K. *FYI on Questions and Answers: Answers to commonly asked "experienced Internet user" questions.* 1991 February; 15 p. (Format: TXT=33385 bytes) (Also RFC 1207)

8. Holbrook, J.P.; Reynolds, J.K.,eds. *Site security handbook.* 1991 July; 101 p. (Format: TXT=259129 bytes) (Also RFC 1244)

9. Malkin, G.S. *Who's who in the Internet: Biographies of IAB, IESG and IRSG members.* 1991 August; 26 p. (Format: TXT=72721 bytes) (Also RFC 1251)

10. Martin, J. *There's Gold in them thar networks! or searching for treasure in all the wrong places.* 1991 December; 27 p. (Format: TXT=46997 bytes) (Also RFC 1290)

11. Lang, R.; Wright, R.,eds. *A Catalog of available X.500 implementations.* 1992 January; 103 p. (Format: TXT=24314 bytes) (Also RFC 1292)

12. Sitzler, D.; Smith, P.; Marine, A. *Building a network information services infrastructure.* 1992 February; 13 p. (Format: TXT=29136 bytes) (Also RFC 1302)

13. Weider, C.; Reynolds, J. *Executive introduction to directory services using the X.500 protocol.* 1992 March; 4 p. (Format: TXT= 9392 bytes) (Also RFC 1308)

14. Weider, C.; Reynolds, J.; Heker, S. *Technical overview of directory services using the X.500 protocol.* 1992 March; 16 p. (Format: TXT= 35694 bytes) (Also RFC 1309)

MaasInfo

The MaasInfo TopIndex files was originally developed by Robert Maas, to provide network users with a single "list of lists." The files have grown to include a bibliography of networking materials, and general information on how to use the networks. The files are available via anonymous FTP from unt.edu (129.120.1.4), in the directory ARTICLES/MAAS/*filename.*

The following descriptions of the MaasInfo files are taken from the MaasInfo.Files document itself.

MaasInfo.Files

This document lists and describes all the MaasInfo files, including latest version identification. This allows you to be sure you are getting the latest version if you are getting the larger files from some other site closer to your location.

MaasInfo.TopIndex

This file is a top-level index to all the major indexes of Internet (and BITNET and Usenet) services, including a description and access information for each index. The indexes themselves cover: interest groups (mailing lists, newsgroups, digests, etc.), special sites (list and file servers, file archives, public-access dial-up hosts, on-line library catalogs, etc.), documents and tutorials (both online and hardcopy) related to these networks. Other top-level indexes available are also included. All the actual indexes and meta-indexes cited are available on the network, accessible by FTP and/or file server. Nearly all are plain text files.

MaasInfo.DocIndex

This file is a bibliography of online documents and tutorials describing how to use various network services, including general network tutorials, glossaries, advice about electronic mail, requesting files indirectly via e-mail, how to get information, Archie file-finding database and service, special interest groups (INFO-NETS, HELP-NET, PACS-L) and their specific collections of documents and archives, services specific to the Internet, some special services, and generally useful reference information.

MaasInfo.HowNet

This file contains very brief information about how to use several very useful network services that are not documented elsewhere, or are documented only in places you might not think of looking or in places that are difficult to access: Internet domain-name to number lookup, BITNET/Internet equivalences, and others.

Lists of Mailing Lists

In Chapter Four, we looked at the various types of mailing lists and electronic conferences on the Internet. These lists number in the thousands, and cover a vast number of topics. Several lists of lists are available on the network to assist network users in identifying and subscribing to appropriate lists.

Internet "Interest Groups" List

A global list of mailing lists, including BITNET and Internet mailing lists, is available via FTP from ftp.nisc.sri.com. The file, called "interest-groups," is in the netinfo directory. It is a very large file (over 500K).

The file is also available via electronic mail. Send a message to:

```
mail-server@nisc.sri.com
```

with the following line in the message body:

```
send netinfo/interest-groups
```

You will receive the file in separate e-mail messages, each containing a moderately sized piece of the larger file.

The list is now searchable as a LISTSERV database, called INTGROUP. It is only available on the LISTSERV at NDSUVM1 (or VM1.NoDak.EDU).

Instructions on searching LISTSERV databases are provided in Chapter Four. An example of a search in the INTGROUP database for a group mentioning "physics" is shown below.

The following lines would appear in the text of a message to LISTSERV@ vm1.nodak.edu (or, on BITNET, LISTSERV@NDSUVM1):

```
//DBlook   JOB   Echo=No
Database Search DD=Rules
//Rules DD *
Select physics in intgroup
index
Select physics in new-list
index
```

These statements would search the local copy of the SRI-NIC Interest Groups (intgroup), and the archives of the NEW-LIST list.

Global LISTSERV List

A comprehensive list of all LISTSERV lists is maintained by the LISTSERV servers. To get a copy of this basic list, which shows only the name of each list on a single line, send an e-mail message to

```
LISTSERV@BITNIC.BITNET
```

with the command

```
LIST GLOBAL
```

in the text of the message. (The LISTSERV software ignores the subject line.)

The global list can also be searched online. Information on searching LISTSERV databases is provided in Chapter Four. An example of a search in the global listing of lists for interest groups on physics is shown below.

The following lines would appear in the text of a message to LISTSERV@ vm1.nodak.edu (or, on BITNET, LISTSERV@NDSUVM1):

```
//DBlook   JOB   Echo=No
Database Search DD=Rules
//Rules DD *
```

```
Select physics in lists
index
Select physics in new-list
index
```

These statements would search the global LISTSERV list of lists (lists), and the archives of the NEW-LIST list.

Usenet Newsgroups

The Usenet News list of groups and mailing lists is available on hosts that run Usenet News or NETNEWS servers, and can be retrieved via anonymous FTP from the pit-manager.mit.edu site. The files are:

netnews.maillist	Usenet News Mailing Lists from news.lists.
netnews.grplist	Usenet Groups from news.lists.
netnews.alternat	Usenet Alternate Groups from news.lists.

Announcements of new newsgroups and mailing lists are posted regularly in the newsgroups news.announce.newusers and news.lists.

Dartmouth Merged List

There is a single file available from Dartmouth that merges the global LISTSERV list and the Internet Interest Groups list. A Macintosh HyperCard application with a user-friendly interface to the list is also available. The simple format of the merged file makes it possible for users to develop their own interface programs as well, in order to adapt the list for use at a local site.

A list of the files available can be obtained by sending an e-mail message to:

```
LISTSERV@DARTCMS1
```

or

```
LISTSERV@DARTCMS1.DARTMOUTH.EDU
```

with the text

```
INDEX SIGLISTS
```

in the body of the message. The files are available via anonymous FTP from dartcms1.dartmouth.edu in the directory SIGLISTS. BITNET users can obtain the files by sending a message to the LISTSERV address above with the command:

```
SEND filename filetype
```

For more information contact David Avery, DAVID@DARTCMS1.BITNET or david@dartcms1.dartmouth.edu.

Directory of Scholarly Electronic Conferences

Diane Kovacs (DKOVACS@KENTVM) maintains an extensive list of scholarly conferences, called the "Directory of Scholarly Electronic Conferences."

The files describe lists on BITNET as well as the Internet. A printed version of this list, called "Electronic Journals, Newsletters and Academic Discussion Lists" is available from the Association of Research Libraries.

The files can be retrieved via anonymous FTP from KSUVXA.KENT.EDU, in the Library directory. They can also be retrieved by BITNET users by sending a message to:

```
LISTSERV@KENTVM
```

with the text

```
GET FILENAME FILETYPE
```

in the body of the message

The files available as of May 1992 are:

Filename	Filetype	Description
ACADLIST	README	Explanatory notes for the directory, with an index
ACADLIST	FILE1	Anthropology-Education
ACADLIST	FILE2	Futurology-Latin American Studies
ACADLIST	FILE3	Library and Information Science-Music
ACADLIST	FILE4	Political Science-Writing
ACADLIST	FILE5	Biological Sciences
ACADLIST	FILE6	Physical Sciences
ACADLIST	FILE7	Business and General Academia
ACADWHOL	HQX	BinHexed, self-decompressing, Macintosh M.S. Word 4.0 document with all six directories
ACADSOCH	HQX	BinHexed self-decompressing Macintosh M.S. Word 4.0 document with the Social Science and Humanities files (1-3)
ACADLIST	CHANGES	Additions, deletions, and alterations

Announcements of New Lists

Those interested in announcements of new mailing lists can subscribe to a mailing list for that purpose, NEW-LIST@VM1.NoDak.EDU (NEW-LIST@NDSUVM1.Bitnet), or the electronic journal NETMONTH (from BITLIB@YALEVM).

To subscribe to NEW-LIST send mail to:

    LISTSERV@vm1.nodak.edu

or

    LISTSERV@NDSUVM1.BITNET

with the body of the mail containing the command

    SUB NEW-LIST *yourfirstname yourlastname*

To subscribe to NETMONTH, send mail to

    LISTSERV@MARIST.BITNET

with the body of the mail containing the command

    SUB NETMONTH *yourfirstname yourlastname*

Library Catalogs

There are hundreds of research libraries—primarily academic, but also public, governmental, and even corporate—that have made their public access catalogs and other resources available over the Internet. However, those wishing to take advantage of Internet library resources face two challenges. The first is finding the network addresses for the libraries, and the second is navigating the interface to each library.

In the sections below, we describe directories that enable you to locate the addresses of library catalogs on the Internet, as well as some software tools that create menu-driven access to the many libraries currently available.

Directories

The two best-known and most comprehensive directories of Internet-accessible libraries are described below. (Please keep in mind that because the files are updated regularly, some of the information about individual files may have changed by the time you read this book.)

Internet-Accessible Library Catalogs and Databases

Prepared and maintained by Art St. George and Ron Larsen, *Internet-Accessible Library Catalogs and Databases* is one of the most comprehensive listings of library catalogs. It also contains information on campus-wide information systems, and even bulletin board systems that are not on the Internet. It includes information on how to access these resources from selected host systems.

This publication is updated periodically. New versions and changes are announced on a number of BITNET lists such as PACS-L, BI-L, CWIS-L and others.

The library catalog sections are divided into those that are free, those that charge, and international (i.e., non-U.S) catalogs; they are arranged by state, province, or country within each section. There is also a section giving dial-up information for some of the library catalogs.

This directory has been criticized because it does not use a standard format for displaying system information; some users feel that this makes it difficult to locate a particular piece of information about a given system. This informal structure, however, does provide more flexibility in the type of information that can be displayed for a given system.

Information provided for most library systems includes basic login information (sometimes a copy of the screen giving system prompts and responses is listed), a contact person, and—in some cases—a description of what the catalog contains.

This directory is available by sending an electronic mail message to

LISTSERV@UNMVM.BITNET

with the following text in the body of the message:

GET LIBRARY PACKAGE

The directory is also available via anonymous FTP from a number of archives, including the LIBSOFT archives at hydra.uwo.ca. (More information on the LIBSOFT archives is provided later in this chapter.)

The directory is updated periodically and announced on a number of BITNET mailing lists, including PACS-L, BI-L, CWIS-L and others. (See the section on "Mailing Lists/Electronic Conferences" in Chapter Four for more information on these lists.)

UNT's Accessing On-line Bibliographic Databases

UNT's Accessing On-line Bibliographic Databases is produced by Billy Barron, systems manager at the University of North Texas, and is often referred to as the "Barron list." This document provides standardized listings for resources in the St. George directory, including the Internet address, login instructions, the system vendor, and logoff information. The arrangement is alphabetic by organization name. An appendix lists the major online public access catalog (OPAC) vendors and provides basic search instructions for each.

Although this directory has the advantage of standardized information formats, it has less flexibility than the St. George list, and thus does not always provide as much information about a given system.

This directory is also updated periodically and announced on library-related listservers. It is available via FTP on the host vaxb.acs.unt.edu (129.120.1.4), in the library directory.

Guide to Using Library Catalogs on the Internet: Selections for Strategies and Use

The Reference and Adult Services Division (RASD) of the American Library Association has produced a guide entitled Library Catalogs on the Internet: Selections for Strategies and Use. This guide provides an overview of using the Internet to reach remote systems, suggests reasons for exploring library catalogs, lists resources for identifying which catalogs are available and for selecting among them, and provides practical tips on navigating the Internet and using unfamiliar systems. It emphasizes a non-technical approach and consolidates information that has been accumulating but has not been available in one source until now.

The guide is available via FTP on host dla.ucop.edu, in directory pub/internet, filename libcat-guide. Printed copies are also available. For more information on obtaining a printed copy, contact RASD at (800) 545-2433, ext. 4398.

Menu-Driven Access

There are a number of programs available that take information from the guides to Internet resources and incorporate it into user-friendly software interfaces that ease the task of connecting to those systems.

Three of these programs are described below. The first, Gopher, is available for a variety of computer sytems. The next two, LIBS and LIBTEL, are designed for use on UNIX-based systems. The last, HYTELNET, will run on both minicomputers and IBM-compatible personal computers.

Internet Gopher
In the "Advanced Applicatons" section of Chapter Four, we looked at the Internet Gopher application as a tool for distributed document delivery. Gopher also allows users to connect to other systems, including library catalogs. Because it hides the Telnet process from the user, it can be an ideal tool for providing library access to Internet users without extensive Telnet experience.

To try using Gopher for library access, follow the instructions provided in Chapter Four for logging into the Gopher system at the University of Minnesota. On the main menu there is a "Library Catalogs" option which takes you to a sub-menu of different library catalogs.

LIBS
The LIBS program, developed by Mark Resmer of Sonoma State University, gives VAX/VMS users a menu of online services, including libraries, campus-wide information systems, and miscellaneous databases.

The systems that LIBS provides access to use different software, and run on different computer systems. LIBS therefore provides system-specific information to users before making the connection to the remote system.

An even more valuable feature of LIBS, is that it provides a single method for quitting form any remote system. By pressing Control +]+Q (or ESC+Q), and then RETURN, the user can quit the Telnet session at any time and return to the LIBS menu.

The opening menu for LIBS is displayed below.

```
LIBS - Internet Access Software v1.3.U (beta)
Mark Resmer, Sonoma State University, February 1992


              Based on data provided by
       Art St. George, University of New Mexico
                 and other sources


On-line services available through the Internet

    1. United States Library Catalogs
    2. Library Catalogs in other countries
    3. Campus-wide Information Systems
    4. Miscellaneous databases
    5. Information for first-time users of this program

Enter the appropriate number followed by RETURN
Press <return> to exit
Enter the number of your choice:1
```

Selecting the first option provides another menu, this one with a listing of all states in the U.S. with Internet-accessible library catalogs. When a state is chosen, yet another sub-menu appears, this one allowing the user to choose from a list of the individual catalogs in that state.

LIBTEL

Another program available for UNIX-based systems is the LIBTEL program. This program provides users with the following opening menu:

Internet Accessible Libraries and Information Systems

(AL)Alabama	(FL)Florida	(LA)Louisana
(AK)Alaska	(GA)Georgia	(ME)Maine
(AR)Arkansas	(HI)Hawaii	(MD)Maryland
(AZ)Arizona	(ID)Idaho	(MA)Massachusetts
(CA)California	(IL)Illinois	(MI)Michigan
(CO)Colorado	(IN)Indiana	(MN)Minnesota
(CT)Connecticut	(IA)Iowa	(MO)Missouri
(DE)Delaware	(KS)Kansas	(MS)Mississippi
(DC)Washington	(KY)Kentucky	(MT)Montana

Internet Accessible Libraries and Information Systems

(NE)Nebraska	(OH)Ohio	(TX)Texas
(NV)Nevada	(OK)Oklahoma	(UT)Utah
(NH)New Hampshire	(OR)Oregon	(VT)Vermont
(NJ)New Jersey	(PA)Pennsylvania	(VA)Virginia
(NM)New Mexico	(RI)Rhode Island	(WA)Washington
(NY)New York	(SC)South Carolina	(WV)West Virginia
(NC)North Carolina	(SD)South Dakota	(WI)Wisconsin
(ND)North Dakota	(TN)Tennessee	(WY)Wyoming
(MISC)Miscellaneous American services		
(bbs)Other Bulletin Boards		
(FOR)Foreign services		

Where would you like to go? [RETURN to exit] CA

As an example, entering "CA" for California provides the following menu:

California

1. Cal Poly State University, San Luis Obispo
2. Melvyl, University of California Online Catalog
3. Gladis, UC Berkeley's catalog
4. California State University, Fresno Agricultural Technology Institute
5. Cal State University, Long Beach
6. Occidental College's Automated Library System

Which number? [RETURN to exit]

Selecting one of these options will open a Telnet connection to the library specified.

HYTELNET

HYTELNET is a hypertext program available for IBM PC, UNIX and VMS systems. It is designed to help computer users who have access to the Internet (via modem, serial line, or direct network connection) reach Internet-accessible libraries, Free-Nets, campus-wide information systems, library bbss, and other information sites via Telnet.

To use HYTELNET on the Internet:

1. Telnet to access.usask.ca (128.233.3.1).
2. Login as "hyTelnet" (no password required).

You will see the following screen:

```
┌─────────────────────────────────────────┐
│   Welcome to HYTELNET version 5.0        │
│   Last Update: April 10, 1992            │
└─────────────────────────────────────────┘
```

What is HYTELNET?	<WHATIS>
Telnet-accessible library catalogs	<SITES1>
Other Telnet-accessible sites	<SITES2>
Internet Glossary	<GLOSSARY>
Cataloging systems	<SYS000>
Understanding Telnet	<TELNET>
Key-stroke commands	<HELP>

```
HYTELNET 5.0 was written by Peter Scott,
U of Saskatchewan Libraries, Saskatoon, Sask, Canada. 1992
Unix and VMS software by Earl Fogel,
Computing Services, U of S 1992
```

Selected Library Systems

Two of the many library systems available over the Internet are described below. These two systems are representative of the types of information available on Internet library catalogs.

Colorado Alliance of Research Libraries (CARL)

The CARL system provides access to member library catalogs (including both public and academic libraries across the United States), current article indexes and document delivery, informational databases (including the Internet Resource Guide and an electronic encyclopedia), and library and system news.

Access to the CARL system is not restricted; however, some databases provided through CARL are restricted to patrons of the member libraries.

Address: Colorado Alliance of Research Libraries
777 Grant, Suite 306
Denver, CO 80203-3580
(303)861-5319

E-mail: help@carl.org

Network Access: Access to CARL databases is available via terminals in member libraries, the Internet and CARL's dial-up modems. (The telephone number is (303)861-1350, and the parameters are 8 data bits, no parity, 1 stop bit. Be sure to turn off flow control and set the end-of-line character to CR only.) Once you are connected to the CARL system, follow the on-line instructions to query the desired database.

MELVYL

The MELVYL catalog is the online union catalog of monographs and serials held by the nine University of California (UC) campuses and affiliated libraries. The

MELVYL catalog also provides access to the current five-year file of the National Library of Medicine's MEDLINE database, which includes article citations and abstracts, indexed from over 4,000 health sciences journals, and to the Institute for Scientific Information's Current Contents file, which contains one year of citations to articles in over 6,500 journals in seven broad subject disciplines. Use of these files, unlike the books and periodicals files, is restricted to the UC community.

Access to the MELVYL online catalog and periodicals file is not restricted. Access to MEDLINE and Current Contents files are restricted under a license agreement to UC faculty, staff, and students.

> Address: Division of Library Automation
> University of California Office of the President
> 300 Lakeside Drive, 8th floor
> Oakland, CA 94612-3550
>
> E-mail: lynch@postgres.berkeley.edu
> Phone: (415) 987-0555 (MELVYL Catalog Helpline)
> Network Access: The system is on the Internet and can be accessed using the host name melvyl.ucop.edu or any of four Internet addresses (31.1.0.1, 31.0.0.11, 31.0.0.13, 31.1.0.11).

Software Archives

In Chapter Four, we discussed the FTP process in some detail. One of the most common uses of FTP is retrieving software from remote sites on the Internet. There are a number of archive sites that maintain large collections of public domain and shareware software. Some of the major archives are described below.

Info-Mac (sumex-aim.stanford.edu)

The Info-Mac archives are maintained at Stanford University. This is one of the largest collections available of software for Macintosh microcomputers.

Almost all files (including programs and other binary files) in the Info-Mac archive are stored in text format. Binary files are almost always converted to text format using the BinHex software described in Chapter Three. It is therefore possible to retrieve most files from this archive

In order to provide a reasonable level of performance and avoid causing Internet overload, the moderators of Info-Mac have imopsed a 35-user limit for anonymous FTP into sumex-aim during working hours (defined as 8amto 5pm Pacific time, Monday through Friday). When this site is busy, it is possible to use one of the many mirror archives around the world (see the descriptions of the SIM-TEL20 and WUARCHIVE sites, below).

A CD-ROM of the Info-Mac archives is commercially available from Pacific Hi-Tech. They can be contacted by phone at 800-765-8369, fax at 801-278-2666, or e-mail at 71175.3152@compuserve.com. The CD-ROM costs approximately $45 including shipping and handling.

(The moderators of the archives warn users that they cannot test software for reliability on all Macintosh configurations. As the software in this archive is generally non-commercial, it may be less reliable and more prone to crashes than many users are accustomed to.)

The Info-Mac Moderators can be reached by sending electronic mail to info-mac-request@sumex-aim.stanford.edu

Library Software Archive (LIBSOFT)

Gord Nickerson, of the School of Library and Information Science at the University of Western Ontario, maintains an FTP archive of library-related software, known as the LIBrary SOFTware Archives. The files are available at hydra.uwo.ca (129.100.2.13) in the libsoft directory.

The LIBSOFT archives do not include general purpose software. The moderator does not attempt to duplicate the coverage of archives like SIMTEL20 (described below). It contains only programs of interest to librarians, and text files intended to help librarians use the Internet.

Descriptions of LIBSOFT files are contained in the text file INDEX.TXT, available in the LIBSOFT directory. Currently the archive is slanted towards MS-DOS. Since the system administrator does not currently have access to other computer systems (such as Macintosh or NeXT computers), this is unlikely to change in the immediate future. Many files are in WordPerfect 5.1 format, but for the convenience of users, the moderator tries to provide ASCII versions as well.

Users are urged not to access this site during local working hours (9am-5pm, Monday-Friday), as it increases the already heavy load on the host computer.

SIMTEL20

A great deal of free public domain and shareware software for the CP/M, PCDOS/MSDOS, Macintosh, and UNIX operating systems, and for the DoD standard programming language, Ada, is available in several archives on WSMR-SIMTEL20.ARMY.MIL (192.88.110.20), a host at White Sands Missile Range, New Mexico. Archives of correspondence for several mailing lists are also available.

SIMTEL20 is a contraction of SIMulation and TELeprocessing, the name of the branch that originally purchased the machine and in whose building the system still resides. The "20" refers to the DECSYSTEM-20 in use at the time the system was named.

The CPM, MSDOS, and MACINTOSH archives are updated frequently with the most recent shareware and public domain software.

The CPMUG, SIGM, and PC-BLUE archives contain software distributed by the CP/M Users Group, the SIG/M Users Group and the PC-Blue Users Group respectively. This software is available on floppy disks from the associated user groups, and the archives are updated as new volumes are issued. The PC-BLUE archive contains software for the IBM PC and similar machines.

The MSDOS archives also contain software for the MSDOS and PCDOS operating systems; but these archives are locally managed, and therefore are updated more frequently than the PC-BLUE archive.

The UNIX-C archive contains a variety of UNIX tools. Those applying specifically to CP/M are in the UNIX-C.CPM directory.

The ADA archive is growing rapidly. Information about this archive is in the ADA.GENERAL directory. In general, the archived software is very good, having been worked over and refined by many users. The documentation and comments tend to be complete and informative.

To obtain directory listings for the various archives, connect to SIMTEL20 via FTP and get these files:

    pd1:<msdos>msdos.crclst
    pd1:<pc-blue>pc-blue.crclst
    pd2:<cpm>cpm.crclst
    pd2:<cpmug>cpmug.crclst
    pd2:<sigm>sigm.crclst
    pd8:<hz100>hz100.crclst
    pd9:<macintosh>macintosh.crclst
    pd8:<misc>misc.crclst
    pd6:<unix-c>unix-c.crclst
    pd7:<ada>ada.crc

There is also a comma-delimited directory listing in each top-level directory, FILES.IDX, which is suitable for importing into a database program. This file may be of greater use than the crclst files because it can be compared against an earlier version of the same file to produce a complete list of files added and deleted from the archives. Using the comma-delimited fields, it is possible to build a script for FTP to maintain a parallel archive. FILES.IDX can be printed or displayed with a simple BASIC program. For more information see the file PD1:<MSDOS.FILEDOCS>AAAREAD.ME.

Copies of correspondence for several mailing lists are kept on SIMTEL20 in directories with names of the form PD2:<ARCHIVES.*KEYWORD*>, where *KEYWORD* indicates the associated mailing list. At present, the following correspondence archives are available:

Mailing List	*Mail Archive Filename*
ADA-SW	PD2:<ARCHIVES.ADA-SW>
AMETHYST-USERS	PD2:<ARCHIVES.AMETHYST>
INFO-68K	PD2:<ARCHIVES.68K>
INFO-APPLE	PD2:<ARCHIVES.APPLE>
INFO-CPM	PD2:<ARCHIVES.CPM>
INFO-FORTH	PD2:<ARCHIVES.FORTH>
INFO-IBMPC	PD2:<ARCHIVES.IBMPC>
INFO-MICRO	PD2:<ARCHIVES.MICRO>

Mailing List	Mail Archive Filename
INFO-MODEMS	PD2:<ARCHIVES.MODEMS>
INFO-MODEMXX	PD2:<ARCHIVES.MODEMXX>
INFO-MODULA-2	PD2:<ARCHIVES.MODULA-2>
INFO-PASCAL	PD2:<ARCHIVES.PASCAL>
INFO-XENIX310	PD2:<ARCHIVES.XENIX310>
INFO-XMODEM	PD2:<ARCHIVES.XMODEM>
NORTHSTAR-USERS	PD2:<ARCHIVES.NORTHSTAR>
UNIX-SW	PD2:<ARCHIVES.UNIX-SW>
VIDEOTECH	PD2:<ARCHIVES.VIDEOTECH>

Washington University (wuarchive.wustl.edu)

Although the SIMTEL20 archives are the originating point for the largest collection of public-domain software, their popularity means that it is often difficult to make a connection to the site. The files at SIMTEL20 are therefore "mirrored" at other sites, so that the software is more easily obtainable.

One of the primary mirroring sites is Washington University (wuarchive.wustl.edu), which keeps copies of all SIMTEL20 files in the mirrors directory. This site also mirrors other archives, including the info-mac archives at sumex-aim.

Directory of Electronic Serials

In the section on electronic mail mailing lists in Chapter Four, we described lists that have evolved into a highly moderated "newsletter" format. The genre of electronic serials includes these newsletters, as well as several other forms of electronically distributed serial publications. These publications are often referred to as "ejournals" or "e-serials," indicating the electronic nature of their form.

The electronic serials available include informal newsletters, formal peer-reviewed academic journals, and non-standard publication formats such as Hyper-Card stacks and digests of mailing list postings.

The Association of Research Libraries (ARL) has compiled The Directory of Electronic Journals and Newsletters, which is intended to provide a comprehensive listing of all journals and newsletters that are of academic interest and available through BITNET, Internet, and any affiliated networks. This directory is part of an ongoing project and is updated as new electronic journals and newsletter come into existence and as existing entries are changed. Every effort has been made to provide the user with up-to-date information. Most entries have been either provided from or scrutinized by the journal and newsletter editors themselves to ensure accuracy.

The primary intent of the directory is to catalog all existing electronic journals and newsletters that are freely available over the various academic networks. A secondary intention is to catalog all e-serials that are being produced over the commercial networks. Thus, over time this directory will provide an entirely comprehensive listing of all e-serials. As the traditional taxonomy of "journal" and "newsletter" is ill-suited to the diversity of formats found within the networks, a third category of "HyperCard Stacks, Digest-Newsletters and Others (Section 4)" is included here.

The ARL directory was compiled by Michael Strangelove, network research facilitator at the University of Ottawa.

Obtaining the Directory in Electronic Form

The directory is currently available in ASCII text from the following location:

1. Contex-L Filelist

   BITNET users can request the files via interactive message by entering the following commands:

   ```
   TELL LISTSERV AT UOTTAWA GET EJOURNL1 DIRECTRY
   TELL LISTSERV AT UOTTAWA GET EJOURNL2 DIRECTRY
   ```

   The files will be sent to the user in NETDATA format.

2. Humanist

   BITNET users can also obtain the files via interactive message by entering the following two commands:

   ```
   TELL LISTSERV AT BROWNVM GET EJOURNL1 DIRECTRY
   TELL LISTSERV AT BROWNVM GET EJOURNL2 DIRECTRY
   ```

   Again, the files will be sent in NETDATA format.

3. ComServe File server
   (Note: The name of the directory files changes to EJournal1 Sources and EJournal2 Sources on the ComServe file server.

   Send an electronic mail message to Comserve@Rpiecs (Bitnet) or Comserve@Vm.Ecs.Rpi.Edu (Internet) with the following command appearing on the first line of the message:

   ```
   Send EJournl1 Sources
   Send EJournl2 Sources
   ```

   No other words, punctuation, or symbols should appear in the electronic mail message. Comserve is an automated system for file retrieval; it will acknowledge receipt of your message and let you know that the files have been sent to you.

Obtaining the Directory in Printed Form

The ARL is the only authorized not-for-profit distributor of print copies of The Directory of Electronic Journals and Newsletters. To obtain a printed version of the directory contact:

Address: Office of Scientific & Academic Publishing
          Association of Research Libraries
          1527 New Hampshire Avenue, NW
          Washington, D.C. 20036
E-mail: ARLHQ@UMDC.Bitnet
Phone: (202) 232-2466
Fax: (202) 462-7849

The publication is available to ARL member libraries for $10 and to non-members for $20 (add $5 postage per directory for foreign addresses). Orders of six or more copies receive a 10 percent discount. All orders must be prepaid and sent to the Association of Research Libraries. Updated editions are planned.

FAQs

Many Usenet newsgroups have developed FAQ—Frequently Asked Questions—documents that contain answers to the questions most frequently asked by new users of those groups. The FAQs often have valuable information for network users, ranging from lists of public access UNIX computer sites (an example of which is provided in Chapter Two) to information on how to obtain electronic mail addresses, and even to trivia on television shows.

The FAQ lists for Usenet newsgroups are stored at two FTP archive sites: pit-manager.mit.edu, and ftp.uu.net. Both sites have a Usenet subdirectory, which has individual subdirectories for each newsgroup with informational postings. In those subdirectories, users will find FAQs as well as other text files of general interest.

There is a WAIS server for these lists, at ftp.uu.net, which allows users to scan for specific information from FAQs even if they do not know which group provides the information. (For more information on WAIS, see the "Advanced Applications" secton of Chapter Four.)

Workshops

One of the most effective ways to train new users in the lore of the network is through workshop presentations. Ideally, workshops will be hands-on, but even without a hands-on component they are an excellent way of presenting Internet concepts.

Finding Speakers

Many librarians and computer specialists active in the network community are willing to present Internet training workshops. Names can often be obtained by posting messages to mailing lists such as PACS-L@UHUPVM1.BITNET, a list addressing automation topics related to libraries, or NETTRAIN@UBVM.BITNET, a list devoted to the topic of training network users.

NYSERNet Workshop Package

NYSERNet, the mid-level regional network serving the New York State area, has created a workshop on the Internet entitled "Beyond the Walls™ Instructional Workshop Package."

This package was originally a day-long workshop co-sponsored by NYSERNet, Inc., and Syracuse University in 1991. The workshop focused attention on the role that networked information can play in a campus environment. It featured nationally-known speakers, an innovative demonstration of network use, and structured group discussions designed to gather strategic information about user needs and activities on campus. The package contains all of the materials needed for another institution to replicate "Beyond the Walls™," including a videotape of the demonstration and a manual highlighting meeting planning, presentations, focus group materials, demo script, follow-up procedures, and a bibliography of key readings. The NYSERNet New User's Guide (described earlier in this chapter) is included in the appendix.

The cost of the workshop package is $49 for NYSERNet(SM) affiliate and interest group members, and $99 for non-affiliates.

Organizations

There are a number of organizations influencing the use and development of the Internet and the National Research and Education Network (NREN). Some of these organizations address policy issues, while others focus on technical aspects of the networks. Some of the major organizations are described below.

Coalition for Networked Information (CNI)

> Coalition for Networked Information
> 1527 New Hampshire Ave, NW
> Washington, D.C. 20036
> E-mail: paul@cni.org
> Phone: (202) 232-2466

The Coalition for Networked Information (CNI) is a joint project of the ARL, CAUSE, and EDUCOM. Their official mission statement includes the following statements:

- The mission of the CNI is to promote the creation of and access to information resources in networked environments in order to enrich scholarship and to enhance intellectual productivity.
- The Coalition pursues its mission by seeking to realize the information distribution and access potential of existing and proposed high-performance computers and networks that support the research and educational activities of a wide variety of institutions and organizations.
- The Coalition accomplishes this realization by undertaking activities, on its own and in partnership with others, that formulate, promulgate, evaluate, and promote policies and protocols that enable powerful, flexible, and universal access to networked information resources.
- The Coalition directs the combined intellectual, technological, professional, and financial resources of its members according to a shared vision of how the nature of information management is changing and will continue to change through the end of the twentieth century and into the beginning of the twenty-first century.

Association of Research Libraries (ARL)

Association of Research Libraries
1527 New Hampshire Ave., NW
Washington, D.C. 20036
E-mail: duane@cni.org
Phone: (202) 232-2466

CAUSE

4840 Pearl East Circle, Suite 302E
Boulder, CO 80301
E-mail: jryland@cause.colorado.edu
Phone: (303) 449-4430

EDUCOM

1112 16th Street, NW, Suite 600
Washington, D.C. 20036
E-mail: kmk@bitnic.bitnet
Phone: (202) 872-4200

CoSN

Mr. John Clement
c/o EDUCOM
1112 16th Street, NW, Suite 600
Washington, D.C. 20036

CoSN is concerned with the implementation and support of networking in K-12 education. Among its activities are:

- Developing and distributing position papers, bibliographies, guides, information packets, and serial publications on K-12 networking.
- Participating in policy discussions on Internet/NREN use.
- Funding released-time grants, travel funds and sabbatical-year fellowships for educators to participate in CoSN activities.
- Encouraging development of better user interfaces and improved access to information, by working with the Internet Engineering Task Force (IETF) Working Group on K-12 user interfaces, developing interface demonstration packets, establishing online directories of K-12 people and resources, supporting the development of resource bases on K-12 networking and related topics, developing a formal liaison to the vendor community, and supporting the development and improvement of user services and training resources.
- Stimulating network-using collaborations and curriculum implementation pilot projects, by securing funding for released-time grants and sabbatical-year fellowships, participating in collaborative studies, and supporting formal liaisons to curriculum groups, disciplinary professional associations, and other communities with interest in K-12.
- Increasing connectivity and lowering connection costs, by supporting direct provision of Internet access in underserved areas, and developing cost/service models for K-12 networking—in collaboration with network providers, telecommunications vendors, and networking experts.

The Electronic Frontier Foundation (EFF)

The Electronic Frontier Foundation, Inc.
155 Second Street
Cambridge, MA 02142
E-mail: EFF@eff.org
Phone: (617) 864 -0665
Fax: (617) 864- 0866

The Electronic Frontier Foundation (EFF) mission statement states that it has been established to civilize the electronic frontier; to make it useful and beneficial not just to a technical elite, but to everyone; and to do this in keeping with society's highest traditions of the free and open flow of information and communication.

Federation of American Research Networks (FARNET)

Laura Breeden
FARNET
100 Fifth Avenue
Waltham, MA 02154
Phone: (617) 890-5120

Federation of American Research Networks (FARNET) is a non-profit corporation, established in 1987 to advance the use of computer networks to improve research and education.

FARNET activities include:

- Offering frequent educational programs for its members.
- Working with other national and international organizations to improve the quality of information and services available to network users.
- Providing information about networking to interested consumers, the media, and decision-makers.
- Negotiating discounts on products and services for its members.
- Providing a forum for the discussion of key technical and policy issues.
- Publishing a monthly online newsletter and regular proceedings of its meetings.

Members of FARNET are local, state, regional, national, and international providers of network services; for-profit and non-profit corporations; universities; supercomputer centers; and other organizations that support the mission of FARNET.

FARNET is governed by a board of directors elected by the membership. Members participate actively in several committees that help direct the activities of FARNET, including technical, program, user services, K-12, nominating, membership, and external affairs.

The Internet Activities Board (IAB)

The Internet Activities Board (IAB) is the coordinating committee for Internet design, engineering, and management. Its activiteis focus on the TCP/IP protocol suite, and extensions to the Internet system to support multiple protocol suites.

The IAB performs the following functions:

- Sets Internet standards.
- Manages the RFC publication process.
- Reviews the operation of its two principal subsidiary task forces, the Internet Engineering Task Force (IETF), and the Internet Research Task Force (IRTF).
- Performs strategic planning for the Internet, identifying long-range problems and opportunities.
- Acts as an international technical policy liaison and representative for the Internet community.
- Resolves technical issues that cannot be treated within the IETF or IRTF frameworks.

Each of the two task forces is led by a chairman and guided by a steering group which reports to the IAB through its chairman. For the most part, a collection of research or working groups carries out the work program of each task force.

All decisions of the IAB are made public. The principal vehicle by which IAB decisions are propagated to the parties interested in the Internet and its TCP/IP protocol suite is the Request for Comments note series and the Internet Monthly Report.

Internet Society

> Internet Society
> 1895 Preston White Drive
> Suite 100
> Reston, VA 22091
> E-mail: isoc@nri.reston.va.us

The Internet Society™ is a professional membership organization created to promote the evolution and growth of the Internet as a global research and education communications infrastructure.

The Society's charter states that it will operate as a non-profit organization for academic, educational, charitable, and scientific purposes among which are:

- To facilitate and support the technical evolution of the Internet as a research and education infrastructure and to stimulate involvement of the academic, scientific, and engineering communities in the evolution of the Internet.
- To educate the academic and scientific communities and the public concerning the technology, use, and application of the Internet.
- To promote scientific and educational applications of Internet technology for the benefit of educational institutions at all grade levels, industry, and the public at large.
- To provide a forum for exploration of new Internet applications and to foster collaboration among organizations in their operation and use of the Internet.

Chapter Six: Policy Issues

There are many policy issues associated with the development of the Internet and the envisioned National Research and Education Network (NREN). These issues are extremely complex, and are often interwoven into extraordinary combinations of legal, educational, and social concerns. This primer concludes with a brief overview of what we feel are some of the most significant issues facing the networking community. We do not pretend to have answers to the questions raised by each of these issues. In fact, it is not clear whether there *are* specific or definitive answers to these questions. It is clear, however, that these issues must be considered by the library and education communities as they venture further into the realm of networked resources.

Six Questions and Grand Challenges

When the High Performance Computing Act of 1991 was signed into law [P.L. 102-194] by President Bush on December 9, 1991, four years of legislative activity came to fruition. In P.L. 102-194, the Director of the Office of Science and Technology Policy is charged to report back to Congress on a set of six points within one year of the enactment. These six points are:

SEC. 102. NATIONAL RESEARCH AND EDUCATION NETWORK.
(g) REPORT TO CONGRESS.—Within one year after the date of enactment of this Act, the Director [of the Office of Science and Technology Policy] shall report to the Congress on—
   (1) effective mechanisms for providing operating funds for the maintenance and use of the Network, including user fees, industry support, and continued Federal investment;
   (2) the future operation and evolution of the Network;
   (3) how commercial information services providers could be charged for access to the Network, and how Network users could be charged for such commercial information services;
   (4) the technological feasibility of allowing commercial information service providers to use the Network and other federally funded research networks;
   (5) how to protect the copyrights of material distributed over the Network; and
   (6) appropriate policies to ensure the security of resources available on the Network and to protect the privacy of users of networks.

It is not clear how long we can expect the Federal government to continue subsidizing the use of and expansion of the existing network. Only a few years ago, it was not certain that the National Science Foundation (NSF) would seek to re-

143

new the contract for the management of the NSFnet backbone. However, many network supporters argued that the network could not continue to be sustained without continued NSF support. As a result, the government announced an open bid for renewal of the contract. The results of a new grant cycle are likely to be announced in 1992, and the responsibility of administering the NSFnet backbone will be continue to be subsidized by the NSF.

Nevertheless, the points delineated in the High Performance Computing Act clearly demonstrate that the Federal government is seeking answers to questions about the commercial applicability of network use. Whether commercial traffic should be allowed to be carried on the network, the suitability of the application of user fees, and a target level for continued Federal investment in the network are all questions which, when answered, could have a tremendous impact on the nature of the existing network. And yet, with the existing political climate in Washington, D.C., there is skepticism on the part of many as to whether the Federal government will support the network indefinitely.

The network is not free! Support of the network at all levels has real financial costs associated with it. Paying the salaries of the people who support the networks, leasing telephone lines for use as network circuits, and purchasing new equipment for upgrading and maintenance of the network all cost real dollars. If the network is to move away from Federal subsidization, what alternatives exist to fill in that gap in funding? Several models of network management have been proposed. Among those models are a commercial free-market economy in which competing service providers seek to outbid each other for provision of service, and a regulated marketplace, similar to that in which the telephone, power, and gas utilities operate.

Counteracting the inclinations of some Federal officials to move the network toward an open commerical market are the many Federal research activities that are dependent upon the uninterrupted availability of network services.

The President, through the Office of Science and Technology Policy, has issued several reports outlining U.S. goals in the area of high-performance computing and telecommunications. The first of such reports, *Grand Challenges: High Performance Computing and Communications*, was released along with the President's budget proposal in February 1991. (A subsequent report, *Grand Challenges, 1993: High Performance Computing and Communications*, was released with the President's 1993 budget proposal.) It outlines a set of computing and communications projects, including global climate modeling, the design of sophisticated massively parallel computing systems, mapping the human genome, and the digital transmission of medical imaging data. These are all applications which are likely to require mammoth amounts of computational power and network bandwidth.

Would the fulfillment of such scientific programs be at risk if the network were to migrate to a commercial environment? That is uncertain, but it seems likely that the presence of these programs offers some stability to the existing support structure for the immediate future.

Topology and Infrastructure

Applications such as those outlined in the High Performance Computing and Communications (HPCC) program have computer and network requirements that differ greatly from the types of applications we have presented in this work. Global weather modeling systems, and raster image processing systems to be used in conjunction with data returned from NASA probes, are applications not particularly well suited to the smaller computing platforms addressed here. This dichotomy between the so-called "high-end" and "low-end" computing applications inevitably generates controversy over the purpose of the Internet and allocation of its resources.

"Data Superhighways" and "The Last Network Mile"

Should the Federal government allocate money for the development of additional backbone bandwidth? Or should Federal tax dollars be spent to develop a widespread data infrastructure to link millions of people to the network from within their homes, their offices, the public schools, and public libraries? Can both areas of network development be addressed simultaneously?

As we explained in Chapter Three, the type of network connection available to the user has tremendous impact on the applications available for use. When you have a TCP/IP connection running directly to your personal computer, you have access to a wide range of network tools and resources not otherwise available. Having your office building wired with fiber optics doesn't really help you if the fiber optic connection stops at the wiring closet. The "last network mile"—an expression referring to the network wiring segment that runs directly to your local computer—will always dictate what you can do with the network and how you can do it.

What is the cost of developing a truly wide-reaching network? The cost must be weighed against the increased personal productivity, enhanced educational systems, and many new jobs that could become a reality if the network is developed at the grass-roots level.

On the other hand, a cure for AIDS might result from the molecular design of a receptor-based drug. The design of such drugs, although not dependent on the network, may be greatly accelerated by the presence of the network. Similarly, what impact will global warming have on our planet? Is there a way to reduce the effects of greenhouse gases? The answers to such questions may be dependent on building a "data superhighway" to allow scientists access to computers and scientific equipment currently beyond their reach. Millions of lives could be changed if scientific programs such as those outlined in HPCC are undertaken with the technology at hand.

Thus, the question raised by these issues is: in these times of limited finances, which is more important to develop—a data superhighway or the last network mile?

Establishing Network Linkages/Gateways

Inevitably, there will be multiple inter-networks in operation at the national back-bone level. In fact, there are already multiple service providers such as Advanced Network and Services, Inc. (ANS), Performance Systems International (PSI), and Alternet competing to provide service at the national level. It is not always clear how the topology of the network will evolve beyond its present form. As we explained in Chapter One, the Internet was originally envisioned to function at three distinct layers: the national backbone, the mid-level/regional network, and the local area network. That topological model of the network, although still widely applicable in many georgraphic areas, we now recognize to be an oversimplified depiction of some rather complicated inter-relationships among public, private, and Federal parties.

Federal Internet eXchange (FIX)

Goods and services produced by the Federal government with public tax dollars belong to the people of the United States. Because large portions of the Internet in the United States have been built with Federal funding, there are many perceived opportunities for conflict of interest if commercial traffic traverses that portion of the network built with public tax dollars. For this reason, and to encourage responsible use of network resources by users, some fairly specific statements pertaining to the acceptable use of the network have been adopted by Federal agencies such as the NSF. Many of the mid-level/regional service providers have followed suit. Below is the NSFnet Acceptable Use Policy:

General Principle:

1. NSFNET Backbone services are provided to support open research and education in and among US research and instructional institutions, plus research arms of for-profit firms when engaged in open scholarly communication and research. Use for other purposes is not acceptable.

Specifically Acceptable Uses:

2. Communication with foreign researchers and educators in connection with research or instruction, as long as any network that the foreign user employs for such communication provides reciprocal access to US researchers and educators.
3. Communication and exchange for professional development, to maintain currency, or to debate issues in a field or subfield of knowledge.
4. Use for disciplinary-society, university-association, government-advisory, or standards activities related to the user's research and instructional activities.
5. Use in applying for or administering grants or contracts for research or instruction, but not for other fundraising or public relations activities.
6. Any other administrative communications or activities in direct support of research and instruction.
7. Announcements of new products or services for use in research or instruction, but not advertising of any kind.

8. Any traffic originating from a network of another member agency of the Federal Networking Council if the traffic meets the acceptable use policy of that agency.
9. Communication incidental to otherwise acceptable use, except for illegal or specifically unacceptable use.

Unacceptable Uses:

10. Use for for-profit activities, unless covered by the General Principle or as a specifically acceptable use.
11. Extensive use for private or personal business.

This statement applies to use of the the NSFNET Backbone only. NSF expects that connecting networks will formulate their own use policies. The NSF Division of Networking and Communications Research and Infrastructure will resolve any questions about this Policy or its interpretation.

The difficulty of policing the network to enforce such policies should not be underestimated. Computers and networking routers operating at the existing level of technology are not at all discerning about the contents of one (or many) of those packets. There is no way, given existing technology, that machinery can determine who is violating such an acceptable use policy as that described above.

In order to lend some order to an increasingly complex network, the concept of a Federal Internet eXchange (FIX) was born. The FIX is a networking organization, designed to facilitate communications, provide interconnection between various Federal networks, and provide operational and technical assistance to its members, who are Federal agencies. The FIX also plays a security role to some degree. By routing network traffic through a highly visible front door, it reduces the likelihood that those interested in violating the acceptable use policy will search for back doors in the network.

Physically, the FIX is a set of computers and routers, each of which is connected to one of several networks operated by a Federal agency. The FIX is the data transfer point for the exchange of data between those various networks. Currently, there are two FIXes in operation. FIX East is operated by SURAnet in College Park, Maryland. It interconnects NSFnet, ESnet (Department of Energy), MILNET (The Armed Forces), The Wideband Net (DARPA), and the NASA Science Network (National Aeronautics and Space Administration). Network links to international operations across the Atlantic are also housed in the FIX East. There is a FIX West in operation at NASA Ames Research Center in California.

Commercial Internet eXchange (CIX)

In Chapter Two, we described the Commercial Internet eXchange (CIX, pronounced "kicks"). The origin of CIX is a somewhat more complicated topic than that of FIX, which was designed primarily as a point of presence for the interchange of packets travelling between different networks. The FIX owes its existence to a practical need for physical links among networks. In contrast, the CIX owes its existence largely to reasons of a political and economic nature. The first

CIX was formed in 1990 by Performance Systems International to trade commercial packets that could not be carried on the NSFnet or other Federally funded networks due to the "acceptable use" policies.

CIX is clearly a play on the acronym FIX, which predated CIX. While the physical locations of the FIXes are with a mid-level regional service provider (SURAnet) and a government network installation (NASA Ames), the CIX locations are located in existing telephone company facilities. CIX West is in operation in the San Francisco Bay area, not far from the FIX West location. A CIX East is currently being planned for the Washington, D.C. area.

If the network is migrating towards existence in a market economy (a topic explored later in this chapter), there is certainly a need for a commercial traffic carrier. However, allowing a single company to transmit and carry commercial traffic in the Internet could provide that company with an unfair competitive advantage in the emerging marketplace. Therefore, CIX was born. Each company building a TCP/IP network can link to the CIX. This commerical infrastructure, being developed by the companies themselves, will allow commercial traffic to be carried to the network.

Where Does the MIX Occur?

You're saying to yourself, "What difference does it make? I don't care whether the packets were passed over the CIX or the FIX, I simply want the information sent to my computer."

At times, it is difficult to determine whether data is commercial in nature or not. When the data originates from different locations, but is received at a single location, both kinds of traffic—non-profit and commercial—ultimately have to cross the same local line in the network. However, separating the data based on its point of origin is what is important. The line at the individual workstation is a baseband line, which is primarily designed to "receive" data. On the other hand, broadband lines at the national backbone level are primarily designed to "transmit" data. Knowing who transmitted the data determines whether it is commercial or not.

The real question concerning FIXes and CIXes lies in, "Where's the *mix*?" At what level of the network topology should transfer of data from the FIX and CIX take place. Should it occur at the backbone? Should the transfer happen in the mid-level regional? Or should individual local area network operators have the choice to operate CIX/FIX gateways for connection to their local organization? What are the operational and fiscal implications in each of these models of the information mix?

For Whom Is the NREN Intended?

There is little doubt that the 1987 NSF Cooperative Agreement between the NSF and Merit Networking, Inc., has had a tremendous impact on the development of packet-switched networking. The growth of the network over the period from 1987 to the present has been phenomenal by any standard of measure: increased packet counts in network traffic; the subsequent expansion(s) of backbone bandwidth at both the national and the mid-level regional levels of the NSFnet to accommodate higher than anticipated network traffic; the many emerging client/server applications, some of which we have described in this book.

But for whom is the network being built? To a large degree, the answer to this question depends upon the person providing the answer. There are many interested parties, who for the most part cooperate in the development of the network. There are times, however, when these various parties have conflicting agendas. It is perhaps wise to recognize that the view of the network, as originally perceived in the world of the DARPA Internet and as proliferated by the NSF, is one of scientists and researchers accessing extremely powerful computers and other peripheral scientific equipment. It was not originally envisioned to be a network to link the nation's research libraries, to carry commercial traffic, or to act as a catalyst for social change.

And yet, those of us observing and participating in the growth of the network see that this change is inevitable: the Office of Science and Technology Policy is already charged with reporting on the mechanism(s) by which the network may be sustained in a free-market, and the library world has been shaken to its very roots with the agents of change entering our homes and offices via two thin copper wires.

Five years ago the problems of academic research libraries were seldom mentioned in a publication such as *The Chronicle of Higher Education*, which represents a broad cross-section of academic affairs. However, in 1992, one is hard-pressed to pick up an issue of *The Chronicle* and *not* find an article about the issues facing libraries. These issues range from the skyrocketing price of serial subscription rates, to the management of copyright and intellectual property rights in an electronic environment, to the announcement of new networked information services by companies as diverse as Dow Jones and OCLC.

The Chronicle itself is participating in a noteworthy experiment in electronic publication. Working in cooperation with the The University Library at the University of Southern California (USC), *The Chronicle* makes electronic copy of each issue available to a team of people working for the The University Library and the USC Computing Center at the time of its print publication. The current issue is loaded into USCInfo (a collection of databases managed using the BRS/SEARCH full-text retrieval system), and is made available to all faculty, staff, and students of USC via the campus network within a few hours of its release in printed form. In fact, John Waiblinger, assistant university librarian for academic information services at USC, has stated publicly that the publication could be online prior to its release in print form, but that due to various political and economic realities the University and *The Chronicle* have agreed to post-publish electronically.

Towards a Ubiquitous Information Infrastructure

Has the USC/*Chronicle* experiment been a success? It may be premature to answer this question completely, but let's consider some statistics. While usage of the *The Chronicle of Higher Education* on the USCInfo system accounted for only three percent of all system use during the months of January and February 1992, thirteen other databases accounted for over fifty percent of the system use. Homer, the USC online library catalog, accounted for forty-two percent of system use, and the remaining five percent is accounted for by use of campus information resources. Increasingly, the traditional online library system, one which provides bibliographic descriptions and local holdings information only, is accounting for a smaller portion of information search and retrieval in academic communities.[1]

One can argue that forty-two percent of all system use is still a substantial amount of usage. Consider, however, another statistic. Of all the searches performed on Homer in February 1992 less than seven and a half percent were performed from a location outside the library building(s) while over ninety-two percent of those searches were performed on internally located terminals. On the other hand, in the same month, nearly twenty-eight percent of all searches performed against the online edition of *The Chronicle of Higher Education* were performed from outside the university library.[2] Can one assume that the catalog is receiving greater usage from within the library because it is being used to locate materials physically housed within it? Why does a resource such as *The Chronicle*, being liberated of its physical limitations, account for more network usage?

Clearly, a common vision is developing in the United States of the network as a purveyor of information. Whether this vision of the network existed in the earliest stages of network development is largely irrelevant. There is a growing community of network users who are fully prepared to store, retrieve, and consume their information in electronic form. The origin of the data is not of interest to this community of users. They perceive the data pipeline to be extant, and are beginning to integrate the bits and pieces of data gleaned from the network into their daily lives.

On June 9, 1992, the front page of *The New York Times* carried the headline "Battle Looms Over Paying to Rewire U.S. for Phones." The article describes the process by which telephone companies nationwide are seeking approval to depreciate their existing copper wire networks at a faster rate than previously anticipated. Telephone companies operate within a regulated industry, and without the approval of Federal and state officials, the telephone companies will be unable to depreciate their existing networks. Telecommunications industry executives, who are feeling increasing pressure from the efforts of the cable television industry to compete for the delivery of broadband network services directly to American homes, are suddenly anxious to develop a fiber optic infrastructure that will also deliver broadband services. *The New York Times* reports:

> Because of recent advances in technology and intensified competition, the phone companies have found their assumptions about the useful life of copper cables are outdated. So they are planning to lay more optical fiber more quickly.[3]

Just a few years ago, telecommunications industry analysts believed that consumers would not bear the increased costs associated with upgrading the pervasive copper network. Now in 1992, however, local exchange carriers across the country are seeking rate increases to replace the existing copper network with fiber optics.

Coincidentally, the same day this story appeared, *The New York Times* carried another front page story reporting the death of William McGowan.[4] Nearly two decades earlier, McGowan, chairman of MCI Communications Corporation, successfully challenged an American Telephone and Telegraph Company (AT&T) monopoly in the telecommunications market. McGowan was joined in a now historic lawsuit by the U.S. Justice Department, and the resulting decision broke AT&T into a major long-distance carrier and several smaller regional carriers. Later, MCI went on to successfully team up with IBM and Merit Networking, Inc., to re-engineer the NSFnet backbone following the 1987 Cooperative Agreement between the NSF and Merit. How ironic that *The New York Times* should report on "recent advances in [networking] technology" on the very day they published McGowan's obituary!

Transformation of the Academic Community

In the last several years alone, great changes in the informal communications process among academics have taken place. The roles assumed by researchers as the network evolves will have a tremendous impact on future evolution of the academic community. The existing network provides scholars, researchers, and students with almost instantaneous access to information in a wide variety of forms. As disciplinary knowlege bases are developed in the network, how will the nature of the academic community be altered?

In the past, philosophical schools have been assembled geographically. In ancient Greece, schools of musical thought in different regions were named after the scalar progressions they used: Dorian, Phyrigian, and Lydian, for example. In Western painting, differing schools centered in places such as the Netherlands, Paris, and London during different time periods. Even in twentieth century America, there are culturally distinct expressions of art which can be traced to specific geographic locations—Country and Western music in Nashville and New Orleans style jazz. What will happen to our communities of academic specialities when the network offers ubiquitous access from any location at any time? Will our schools, and their works, become centered in a segment of "virtual space" in the network?

Another question to be considered is what role the network will play in the traditional processes of academic publication and instruction. Already, new methods of "distance learning" are being made possible through the use of electronic networks. What effect will the networks have on the manner in which scholars exchange their publications?

Access to Networked Information

If we assume that we are moving towards the development of a medium that will provide uniform access to information in this country (and, for that matter, worldwide), then we must address the issues associated with access to information within that networked environment. Depending on who you are, who you work for, and where you are located, the barriers facing you in accessing the current network may be many or few. The network playing field is not a level one at this time. The stability of the environment may come into question soon, as well also. There are many factors in play, each of which is subject to volatile change.

Nevertheless, it is apparent that the developing environment is one which people are interested in using. Individuals and institutions want to know how they can connect to the network, and they want to be free to explore the resources that the network has to offer. As the network marketplace matures, and more people become reliant upon the services offered in the network, we can expect to see an increasingly structured environment develop. The effects of the imposition of this structure on the network and its users cannot yet be determined. The development of emerging network policies will shape the future of access to networked information.

Barriers to Access

Certainly, librarians understand the apparently widening gap between information "haves" and information "have-nots." To many in the information professions, it appears that there is a vast social change taking place—a change that may be leading to the development of a permanent information underclass. There are many barriers to be overcome in the development of a sustainable network marketplace. Overcoming these and other potential barriers is one of the greatest challenges facing our society as we attempt to develop a ubiquitous information infrastructure.[5]

Education of the User

In the existing marketplace, the single greatest barrier to the achievement of access to the network and the resources contained therein may be the potential network user's level of understanding regarding connection options. Currently, there are many opportunities for those interested in accessing the network to achieve connectivity. Indeed, the opportunity for connection may never again be as great as it currently is or has been over the past several years. Federal subsidization of network development at the national and mid-level/regional level has presented tremendous opportunities for interested parties. What keeps many potential network users from "plugging in" is not necessarily a lack of opportunities, but rather a lack of *knowledge* of those opportunities.

However, even if an individual or an organization has acquired a reliable method of network connectivity, there are still tremendous educational barriers to be overcome on the part of the individual user. Knowing what is available in the network, and knowing how to navigate within the network, are more than minor barriers to accessing information. The needed educational tools are beginning to emerge. Unfortunately, many of those tools have only been accessible to those who already had the skills to find and retrieve them from the network—a rather circular process. This book is one of the growing number of sources intended to present educational opportunities for those not yet conversant in the legend and lore of the networked world, without first requiring those skills of its readers.

The High Cost of Technology

There is a potentially lucrative market in the provision of educational training services to network users. As advanced technologies mature within the network marketplace, we hope that there will be a corresponding drop in the sheer volume of material users need to know in order to productively use the network. The development of advanced network agents (such as those described in Chapter Four, under "Advanced Applications") will to a large extent shield the user from the contrived languages of networking protocols. Similarly, an increasingly sophisticated network support infrastructure should improve the exchange of information between those who develop tools in the network and those who are interested in using them.

The development of advanced tools, the maintenance of a support infrastructure, and the physical operation of backbone network interconnection do not come without cost. In fact, these costs can be quite substantial. Those who subsidize such activities therefore have good reason to expect a return on their investment. The real costs associated with building and maintaining the network must ultimately be borne by the consumers in the marketplace. Similarly, there is a cost associated with hardware and software, and the user is expected to bear this as well. A high bandwidth network connection coming into the home or office is useless without a computer to connect to it; the user will need to purchase that computer.

One of the critical issues facing many higher education institutions today is the maintenance of a consistent computing and networking infrastructure within the organization. The expected life span of the technology being purchased is shrinking rapidly. Computing industry analysts believe that the rate of technological turnover within the industry is roughly thirty months. Manufacturers recognize that the consumer is unwilling, or unable, to bear the cost of replacing their computing hardware or software every thirty months, and plan the depreciation of their products over a longer cycle. However, products become outdated before that cycle ends due to research and development breakthroughs within the industry.

The majority of colleges and universities make computing equipment purchases from one-time capital expenditures. Institutions are only beginning to recognize that purchases of computing and networking products are recurring costs associated with the maintenance of a productive campus computing environment, rather than single expenditures made when surplus money is available. Development of a strategic plan to ensure for the provision of a competitive computing environment in any organization, academic or otherwise, is necessary.

The results of this rapid technological obsolescence are evident in most existing automated library systems. Because automated library systems process such large amounts of data, these systems have historically been designed using a large central processing facility—a machine such as a mainframe or minicomputer, supporting multiple terminals. The "line mode" terminals employed in these systems, however, are not capable of supporting more advanced client/server applications within the libraries. Although these systems have a place in the world of networked information, their technology is not suitable for handling multimedia information. If an academic library hopes to compete for the role of delivering multimedia information on campus, strategies for updating the computing and networking infrastructures in libraries must be implemented. And, of course, with a thirty-month life expectancy likely for the technology, the timing of decisions to upgrade substantial amounts of computing equipment must be carefully considered.

For the individual consumer, the costs associated with establishing a network connection may seem overwhelming. However, one must consider the application of other similar technologies to one's everyday life. Few homes in this country do not have at least one television, and a significant portion of those homes receive their television transmission via a cable carrier. What auto manufacturer (or dealer) would try to sell a car without a radio? In fact, the majority of cars in this country are sold with FM stereo. However, there was a time when an AM radio was was an expensive luxury in an automobile.

As technology matures, costs of production tend to drop. When the cost a consumer will bear for a product aligns with the costs of manufacturing the product, in such a way that the manufacturer can make a profit, a market is created. Such a market for networked information is currently emerging. However, we recognize that the costs associated with entering the networked information marketplace are still substantial—and even prohibitive—for many individuals and organizations at this time.

Ownership of Data

The unseen bits and gigabytes travelling the networks are not information, they are data. Data is meaningless; it has no value. That is, it has no value until such time as it has been received and understood by an individual. When understanding (i.e., learning) takes place, the data is transformed into information. Any value associated with the data is meaningful only when placed within the context of a user. How much value does a user place on the data? In what form can that value be measured? Increasingly, our society views data as a commodity that can be bought and sold. It may be that in the post-industrial era—after it has become too expensive to manufacture goods produced in first-world markets where there are high costs associated with the first-world labor force—the buying and selling of data will sustain the economy. The cost of data is closely associated with the high costs of technology.

It has been said that money is power. If we are willing to pay for data, then does not the person, or organization, owning the data also possess power of a sort? Certainly, if the owner of the data seeks to maximize the return on his/her investment in the data by charging the highest price the market will bear, then data ownership could prove to be highly lucrative in situations where data is highly coveted. Unfortunately, the logical, unrelenting nature of computers and networks—tools specifically designed to facilitate the transmission, duplication, and manipulation of data—to a large degree discourages the interests of limited access, for-profit, data ownership.

This opposition between the nature of computers/networks and the treatment of data as a commodity that can be bought and sold has significant implications related to the provision of commercial information delivery services in the network. Most companies that depend on the selling of data for their livelihood are intrigued by this emerging marketplace and the opportunities it offers. Yet, at the same time, they are concerned that data introduced into the network will undermine their ability to sustain multiple and repeated sales. Computer software manufacturers and the recording music industry have already suffered such losses due to the unauthorized duplication of their wares in foreign countries where the local governments are either incapable or unwilling to enforce the violation of the rights associated with ownership. The chief right associated with such ownership is a fair return, or a royalty, for the use of that data.

Copyright and Intellectual Property

Some argue there are no rights associated with data ownership. Instead, companies providing data delivery for a fee are actually selling a service. The data itself is not the focus of ownership, rather it is the value added to that data when it is provided through the service of a company. Unfortunately, this view, no matter how intriguing it may appear, is in direct conflict with copyright law and the laws governing transfer of intellectual property rights in this country.

The existing copyright code in this country (a convention shared by a large number of developed countries) is widely considered to be insufficient to handle the complexities presented by innovative new technologies. Although this may be true, there is also a growing recognition in this country that there is not likely to be any significant revision to the laws governing copyright and intellectual property in the foreseeable future. A number of organizations (such as the Coalition for Networked Information [CNI] and the Electronic Frontier Foundation [EFF]) recognize that solutions to ownership rights, intellectual property, and copyright in the networked marketplace need to be developed without substantial changes to existing legislation or practice, and are actively engaged in programs toward that end.

In particular, CNI is engaged in a project called the Rights for the Electronic Access to and Dissemination of Information (READI). Through a series of expert panels, READI is attempting to define an environment that will be acceptable to the owners of data, the consumers of data, and the intermediaries who provide for the transfer of data from the owners to the consumers. One panel will explore the networked marketplace from the perspective of data owners. Another panel will pursue the definition of an acceptable market for the consumers of data. A third panel, made up of representatives from both the owners and consumers will attempt to build a model of networked information delivery which accommodates both points of view. CNI hopes that models for networked information delivery developed through the READI program will be implemented, at least in prototype systems, within the network in the near future.

To Regulate or Not to Regulate

If it is true that data is a commodity, then it seems possible that a monopoly on a specific genre of data could be secured in the information marketplace. In fact, there are publishers in the print marketplace that have been accused of just such an effort. Theoretically, competition in the marketplace plays a role in maintaining lower costs and it also provides the consumer with a wider variety of product offerings. However, when a single organization or individual owns the vast majority of resources in a single marketplace, a monopoly ensues which can prevent fair competition from occurring.

Consider the ramifications of a single publisher securing the rights to all medical journals. Doctors and medical researchers who are reliant upon the data contained within the databases and printed publication of this company would be forced to pay whatever price the company charged for the data. Information related to the development of new drugs to treat diseases such as AIDS and cancer and the expeditious reporting on new treatment methods for those diseases could be hindered as a result of such a monopoly. If the doctors and researchers do pay the higher prices, the costs are ultimately passed on to the patients who seek treatments.

Antitrust legislation is designed to prevent just this type of occurrence in any given marketplace. Such antitrust action was successfully leveraged against AT&T in 1974 by William G. McGowen, then chairman of MCI Communications Corporation. The resulting decision—which supported McGowen's claims that AT&T possessed an unfair advantage in the telecommunications market—has allowed the emergence of the multiple service providers within the mid-level/regional Internet networks. Are these service providers themselves subject to antitrust legislation? The Federal government has taken significant actions to ensure the emergence of competing service providers in the high-speed networking arena. It is unclear, however, how existing antitrust legislation applies to the issue of ownership of data.

The degree to which the Federal (and/or State) government should regulate the development of the networked marketplace is a topic of considerable debate. Some argue that network service providers should be regulated in the same manner as utilities companies, in order to guarantee the provision of a service they believe to be fundamental. Critics of this view argue that such regulation is unwarranted, and that fair competition in the marketplace will ultimately better suit the needs of the consumer by providing more choices. Determining the optimal balance between regulation and free trade is not likely to be resolved in the immediate future.

Quality Control of Electronic Data

The application of quality control to data is another issue facing the development of a networked information market. In the existing network, it is difficult to determine the quality of the information obtained from the data at hand. Admittedly, the traditional print market has had its share of poor-quality publications. Overall, however, the print publication industry has provided, and continues to provide, high-quality information products. Ensuring the same level of quality through the electronic dissemination of information via networks may require the development of new procedures to ensure quality control.

The Editorial Process and Peer Review

One of the primary tools employed by those competing in the print market to ensure quality of publications is the editorial process. Very few printed publications reach the marketplace without being subjected to the scrutiny of editorial reading and comment. Often, a publication will go through several iterations of editing before arriving in classrooms and the shelves of bookstores and libraries. A spouse, a friend, or a colleague may read the work, and offer feedback to the author which may result in reworking the material. Most assuredly, the publisher employs the services of one or more professional editors who will read the book. Some editors will check the content of the book, reviewing its applicability for the publisher's readership niche. Copy editors will read a work for grammatical and spelling errors. Eventually, the author is presented with an opportunity to re-read and make final corrections to the work before it is actually printed.

This degree of review typically does not occur with "publications" over the network. In fact, many documents disseminated through the network for public consumption have not even been read by anyone but the author before being launched into the network. Such is the nature of low-cost electronic distribution

One can readily argue that the activity occurring on such lists is not "publication proper." Nevertheless, electronic mailing lists provide at least one function in academic communities similar to that of printed journals. They provide an individual with an opportunity to expose thoughts, theories, and ideas to a group of his/her peers for comment and consideration. Letters to the editor, and other similar columns in print publications, have filled this role in the past. Electronic mailing lists have been described as electronic "town squares," interactive letters to the editor, and ongoing panel discussions.

Not all electronic publications use such informal structures, however. As we described in Chapter Five, an increasing number of electronic journals and newsletters are employing a more formal editorial structure. These electronic publications—such as the University of Houston's *Public Access Computing Systems Review*—more closely resemble their print counterparts.

There are many advantages for authors who choose to disseminate their work electronically on the network. Since the material can be processed electronically, databases of references can be easily compiled for future reference. Networked delivery also offers the potential of reaching a relatively large audience almost instantaneously, and with very little direct cost to the producer and distributor.

Rapid dissemination of information is, of course, the main advantage provided by the network. This rapid dissemination conflicts directly with the editorial process. Subjecting a work to repeated reviews before releasing it to the network would greatly increase the time required for delivery. For some members of the networked community, this time lag is not justifiable; they would prefer to have the information delivered rapidly and to subsequently make their own determination regarding its quality. This places the burden of "weeding" for quality control upon the shoulders of the information consumer. If this editorial practice (or lack thereof) is to continue in the networked information environment, will new methods need to be employed to accommodate the differing environment?

Peer Review and Collection Development

Another process employed by libraries to guarantee the quality of materials maintained for the community of users is that of collection development. Librarians, relying on their knowledge of the print marketplace, and using additional input from the peer review process (book reviews, faculty recommendation, and the librarian's own subject expertise) make determinations about the purchase of materials best suited to the needs of the library's community of users.

The publication explosion in the print market over the past several decades, coupled with shrinking library budgets and economic inflation, has greatly complicated the collection development process. Budgetary restrictions force libraries to purchase no more than a fraction of the available materials in any given area. This is complicated by the fact that libraries are now collecting multimedia materials such as videotapes, compact discs, films, and electronic data, in addition to the traditional books and journals. Inevitably, the collection development efforts of the library staff are insufficient to meet the needs of all users, and conflicts result over materials which the library lacks. Nevertheless, the majority of the user community benefits from a process they often do not even recognize to be occurring.

Many of the nation's leading research libraries have focused their collection development on specific topical areas, building unique and valuable collections in those areas. Most large academic libraries, and many of the largest public libraries, have one or more such collections. Researchers and academics worldwide flock to these libraries to use these special collections. As the Internet improves the ability of libraries to share their resources, libraries may become increasingly specialized, relying on each other to meet their patrons needs. The collection development process already in place will need to become even more sophisticated, in order to ensure that materials are collected in a way that will best suit the needs of library users.

Manual Data Processing vs. Automated Data Processing

Hand in hand with the issues of editorial practice and collection development go a host of questions related to the methods of data processing typically employed by libraries. Typically, the data made available to users in online public access catalogs (OPACs) and other online systems has been compiled manually. There is a growing recognition in the networked community that such compilation of data is time consuming, and that it may not offer significant advantages in the storage and retrieval of electronic information. Library descriptive cataloging procedures are based on the need to create finding aids that offer the library user a method of searching for and retrieving printed information. Abstracting and indexing procedures were developed to concisely describe printed source documents of much greater scope and magnitude. Theoretically, the brief record created is a microcosm of the larger work, and adequately describes its nature and content. Classification schemes are imposed on materials in an effort to present them to library users in an organized fashion.

Advances in automated data processing provide new opportunities for the storage and retrieval of text (and other media). Computers can quickly and easily create sorted indexes containing entries for each word in a textual document. Operations once prohibitively expensive to perform on computers are easily accomplished today. Computing capacity available only through central processors beyond the means of entire universities twenty years ago is now affordable in computers designed for individual use. The average monthly family phone bill is likely to be more expensive than a one megabyte memory chip. Magnetic disk drives, although more expensive, are available in a wide variety of sizes and an equally distributed price range. For the price of an average family car, an individual could equip a computer with a data storage capacity of several gigabytes.

However, the greatest costs associated with textual data processing are often not the computers used in the processing, but rather the labor required to convert printed material into machine-readable form. Manual input of textual information is still quite expensive. For this reason, most writers working in 1992 are probably using a computer and word processing software to create their work. In fact, many publishers now require writers to submit their work in machine-readable form; this saves them the considerable cost of having the manuscript converted into an electronic format.

In earlier portions of this book, we have tried to show the potential networks offer for the widespread distribution of textual material. An infrastructure is developing that will someday allow entire books to be moved between any two people in this country. In fact, entire books are already being exchanged in the existing network. There are no fewer than three electronic editions of the Bible available at various network locations. Michael Hart's Project Gutenberg (described more fully in Chapter Five) is rapidly accelerating the process whereby printed materials residing within the public domain are converted to machine-readable form. If solutions to the problems associated with copyright and intellectual property in an electronic environment can be found, publishers will have an incentive to provide their publications in electronic form over the network. In fact, as we have noted, publications such as *The Chronicle of Higher Education* are already doing so.

This has tremendous implications for libraries. If data already exists in a form which can be readily recognized by machines, and if high-speed networks are emerging to transport this information into our homes and offices, how can libraries justify their continued practice of managing and distributing information? Librarians cite two reasons: first, that the networks are in a transitional period, and there is a need to maintain existing systems until a more modern system can be developed; and second, that the new networked systems present users with a problem in identifying and retrieving information (an area known in the library profession as "precision and recall"), and that librarians will therefore be needed to provide intermediary services.

The first argument is clearly convincing. If libraries are expected to continue serving their patrons, they must maintain their existing systems while new methods of information delivery are developed. (Of course, this does not take into account the difficulties in maintaining the old system and developing a new system on an already shrinking budget.

The second argument is not as clear-cut. Many librarians argue that existing processes of descriptive cataloging, abstracting and indexing, and classification offer mechanisms that aid the precise retrieval of data from within large electronic databases. The maintenance and application of controlled vocabulary (also known as thesaurus) terms to data in electronic databases is not always efficient. An average descriptive cataloging record contains two to four of these subject headings. If librarians were free to spend more of their time applying principles of library science to the database records being created, and less time doing data entry, it is quite likely that the results of recall and precision studies would be different. Many traditional library procedures, such as the creation of "authority lists" to provide consistency in the citing of personal names, are equally if not more valuable in today's database technology.

Managing Data in Its Original Format

Can a lesson in data management be gleaned from the existing network? Experience dictates that it is possible, to some degree, to build very usable databases consisting of textual data in its original, unstructured form. Several systems employed in the network, most notably the Wide Area Information Server (WAIS) system, are based on this philosophy. Data gathered from a wide variety of sources on the network is routinely loaded into WAIS databases, without the need for any significant pre-processing.

There are disadvantages to using unstructured data. For example, WAIS is currently unable to interpret the difference between a record containing the full text of a document and a record containing only a bibliographic citation to that document. However, there are many advantages to be had from employing this method of text management. Most importantly, the costs associated with building databases are greatly reduced if no pre-processing of the document is required.

One thing seems evident: libraries are unlikely to be able to impose any requirements for the structuring of distributed network data on network users. The resulting implication is that libraries wishing to develop comprehensive collections of data distributed over the network will have to learn to manage the data in the form it is presented. This is not to say that all data in the network is unstructured. Indeed, the management of data distributed by electronic mail lists is greatly simplified by the existence of a standard RFC822 header (as discussed in Chapter Three). Similarly, standards being developed by the Internet Anonymous FTP Archives (IAFA) working group of the Internet Engineering Task Force (IETF) are likely to facilitate the automated management of FTP archival data.

We believe librarians will have to confront the fact that the data of value to their user communities will not always be neatly packaged in the MARC format (a standardized data format widely used in library online catalogs). Instead, it is time for the library profession to develop of information systems that can accommodate data in its native format.

Archival Storage of Electronic Information

Even if all the problems associated with the development of systems and procedures for dynamic networked information systems are overcome, there will still be issues related to the archival storage of electronic information that need to be addressed. Currently, the data being created and stored on the network is rapidly exceeding the capacity of the computers on the network. What policies are being employed to ensure that data which may be of use to future generations is being preserved?

The Loss of Data

The ultimate cost of processing electronic data for the network is still an unknown quantity. At times, it appears that our ability to gather data greatly exceeds our ability to analyze and interpret the data. Consider a typical transaction log from an online information system. It is possible to trap all the keystrokes of every user of an online system, and to collect information such as the time the user logged onto the system, the time the user logged off, and the databases accessed. It is possible to determine quite a bit about the nature and needs of the user population by examining this activity log. The trouble with most of these logs, however, is that they can generate far more information in a matter of hours than the typical researcher can analyze in several months. Does that mean that the data is not useful? At some point it may be invaluable to a researcher. However, it is more likely to be erased without a second thought. How much data is being discarded daily because there is insufficient storage space for it?

Beyond transaction logs, one day there may be remote sensing equipment tied into the network. These sensors will provide updates on all manners of data: current weather data from Boston, readings from the ongoing partical physics experiment in Texas, news (and perhaps video) feeds from news services such as the Associated Press and Cable News Network. All the network user will need to do is "tune" his/her computer into the proper network frequency, and voilá—instant data. How will we archive these ongoing data streams?

Advances in technology also add to the problem of potential data loss. Current standards for processing data may be outdated in a few years. The punch card and punch tape serve as examples. At one time in the history of data processing, both of these forms were commonly used to store programs and data, as well as to input code and data into computers. If a set of punch cards turned up in your office tomorrow, however, would anyone have the equipment to determine what they contained? They might not even be recognized as a data storage mechanism!

Another factor in data loss is data that has been copied to magnetic tapes during system backups. Over the past decade, advances in magnetic tape technology have made older tape machines obsolete. Data stored on tape using these systems is not compatible with new tape units, so the older machines must be maintained. Even if the older tape machine is still in working order, it may not be possible to connect it to the more advanced computers used in the future. The transfer of megabytes or even gigabytes of data from old tapes to a new format is often not considered cost-effective, and the old tapes are often discarded. Along with the tapes goes the data they contained—lost forever.

This phenomenon of "technology dinosaurs" poses problems for the long-term storage of electronic data. It is true that most equipment manufacturers try to provide migration paths for their users, enabling them to transfer data from one generation of computers to the next. But nearly everyone who has moved from one computer system to a newer one has a floppy disk or two sitting around with data that was never converted for use with the existing equipment. There is no reason to believe that this problem will ease as advances in computers arrive with more frequency.

Another aspect of data loss involves large disk storage spaces. When hard drives on personal computers were relatively small—in the neighborhood of 10 to 20 megabytes—utilities showing a simple directory listing (e.g., the DIR command in DOS, or ls in UNIX) were suitable for browsing through data hierarchies. However, as the average size of hard disk drives has grown, so has the difficulty of using these tools. Hierarchical arrangements of data have become complex, and are really impractical for managing large amounts of data. More advanced finding aids (e.g., grep in UNIX, and Find File for the Macintosh operating system) were needed. But even those tools have limits. Today, it is not uncommon to find personal computers with disk drives several hundred megabytes in size.

Browsing through data stored hierarchically on these large storage units is impractical. Tools that search for text strings within the files stored on large disk units are inefficient, and can use a considerable amount of processing power that would be better spent on other tasks. More sophisticated methods of tracking data within storage units are needed, or data will be lost to users because it cannot be quickly and easily retrieved.

The Problem of Data Remanance

Perhaps a greater problem than that of loss of data is the problem of data excess or data remanance. When data is duplicated and distributed throughout the network, it is virtually impossible (given the limits of today's networking technology) to ensure that the data will be destroyed, even if that is the wish of its creator. For example, an author may wish to destroy an older edition of a work when a newer edition is released. Except for a few copies of his/her work that will be saved for archival purposes, the author may wish to destroy older editions to make sure they are no longer distributed in the network as they contain information which is now out of date. This is not currently possible.

Let's look at an example. Several years ago, a news posting appeared on many networks and bulletin board systems, warning users of impending Federal legislation intended to place a tax on the use of modems. A computer user who had learned of this ill-conceived legislation had used the network to alert other computer users. Although the legislation was eventually withdrawn, this same posting reappears regularly on various electronic forums, each time reposted by a newly alarmed networker who encountered the notice for the first time. One can assume that other "urban legends" have been created and sustained with far less exposure than this ill-fated note.

As another example, when librarians make a determination that a book is no longer pertinent to the needs of the library's users, they may choose to remove the work from the library's collection. Such a process is termed "weeding" the collection. With machine-readable data, which is far less tangible than a book, there is a tendency toward passive acceptance of unnecessary data. Rather than risk losing a piece of data into the the "noise" of the network, users have a tendency to latch onto it and retain it. In what manner will the electronic weeding of our growing databases occur? The potential system maintenance problems presented by data remanance are at least troublesome as those of data loss.

Roles

The emergence of a new network marketplace has resulted in new jobs, new opportunities, and new roles for those closely affiliated with the network. It also offers many opportunities for existing roles to be redefined. Librarians, computer scientists, educators, and managers—among others—can play a vital role in designing new tools for networked information delivery, and in shaping the new processes associated with the use of those tools. Each of these vocations has skills required to fill roles in the emerging network marketplace.

These diverse disciplines may merge to create a new professional—one who understands computers and networks, who can apply the tools of data organization to networked information, who understands how people learn, and who has the business savvy to provide those services in an open and competitive market. Or we may see the creation of new interdisciplinary teams working cooperatively to tackle the challenges presented in the network.

The Librarian

The role of the librarian is likely to undergo tremendous change in the coming era of networked information. Computers and networks are presenting significant challenges to the nature of libraries as we know them. The widespread availability of printed books brought enlightenment to the western world. Similarly, the radio, the telephone, and the television have had an impact on the way mankind communicates. However, none have had such an impact on the way people communicate as the printed word, that is until the network.

The written word is a major carrier of knowledge in our world. Today, the network offers a tremendous opportunity for interactive sharing of written information. In the future, it will also provide a vehicle for the interactive delivery of visual materials. Television and radio have had a lesser impact on learning because they are not interactive in nature. Effective education using the written word requires active participation on the part of the learner. The network provides new opportunities for interactive education, and challenges librarians to undertake the management of the collective sum of human knowledge at a previously unimaginable level.

Information Intermediaries

Throughout history, and especially in recent decades, the librarian has assumed a role as gatekeeper to information. Although the ethics of the library profession dictate equal access to all information for all people, librarians have played an increasingly important role in providing directed access to information. Throughout the 1970s and the 1980s, librarians have assumed a role as intermediaries between the researcher and data contained in online databases such as those popularized by DIALOG and BRS. Whether this role of information intermediary is likely to increase or decrease with the popularization of the network is difficult to determine.

Certainly, the network provides opportunities for the end-user to access data much more directly than was possible in many traditional systems of library organization. Already a wide range of products have been introduced into the marketplace based on the premise that the owners of data should sell information directly to the consumer. Terminology such as "digital librarian" has become commonplace in advertisements for these products. Clearly, some researchers have grown to believe that librarians as intermediaries serve to restrict access to information at least as much as they enhance such access. Such sentiment has fostered the development of tools designed to assist end-users in directly searching databases (one example of such a tool is the National Library of Medicine's popular Grateful Med product).

On the other hand, the complexity of the existing networked information environment may create an even greater need for full-time information professionals. Users may not be aware of all relevant information in this increasingly complex environment, and may overlook critical data. Information professionals who take pro-active measures to promote their services may actually thrive as a result.

Organizer of Data

The librarian also plays a significant role in the organization of data. Current technology still requires that a considerable effort be expended in structuring data in large databases so as to achieve maximum efficiency in storage and retrieval. However, in the long term, much of the activity related to data structuring/ organization currently performed by librarians may be performed through automated processes in a distributed environment. Certainly, existing levels of data processing technology allow for the management of data in far less structured forms than those typically employed within the library community. There appears to be an emerging trend toward the management of raw data through technology rather than human intervention.

The development of the Human Genome Database at Johns Hopkins University, a project pairing the abilities of the librarians with the knowledge of medical researchers, is a successful example of an innovative approach to data management. Medical researchers chose to work with librarians in the management of data generated through research findings rather than to attempt to analyze the data and then publish the results. The project has resulted in the creation of a widely acclaimed database of human genetic data. Richard Lucier, university librarian and associate vice-chancellor for academic information management at the University of California, San Francisco, worked on the Human Genome Database. He describes the approach to data management employed in this project in the "knowledge management" model.

In the traditional print marketplace, the librarian's role in the publication process follows the report of research findings at conferences and publications in the print marketplace. However, in the knowledge management model, the involvement on the part of librarians occurs at a much earlier stage in the scholarly communications process. The researcher turns raw data over to the librarians who, in turn, build the information system from the raw data. The researcher analyzes the data, possibly with the assistance of data analysis tools integrated into the information system itself. At a much later stage the researcher reports findings in print

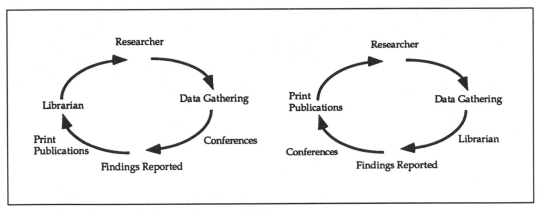

Figure 7. Organization of roles and responsibilities.

publications. Consider the roles and responsibilities of a professionally trained librarian as reflected in each of the two models of scholarly communications shown in Figure 7.

Knowledge management has been criticized as being inapplicable to certain types of data-gathering processes, especially those frequently employed in the social sciences. However, it is clear that knowledge management is an innovative approach to the management of raw data. Such processes as knowledge management—processes assuring that data is organized and stored in machine-readable form, with print publication becoming a byproduct of that process—will be critical if the promise of networked information is to be fulfilled.

The Computer Scientist

The current complexity of the network assures a continuing role for the computing professional into the foreseeable future, and beyond. To return to the analogy of the automobile, it may be true that no understanding of the internal combustion engine is necessary to drive an automobile, but some person or persons knowledgable in metallurgy, combustion physics, and mechanical engineering was needed to design and build such a device. The same is true of the network. Computing professionals will be required to maintain the interconnections of the network, design new tools for use on the network, and train users in the use of the network.

Network Management

It is surprising how few people understand the amount of labor required to maintain network operations. The network does not run itself! All of the mid-level regional service providers have network operations centers acting as the central nervous system for the network. When a circuit goes down, people are available to trace the problem and correct it. As more sites become inter-connected to the network, there is a tremendous opportunity for growth within the organizations of these service providers.

Additionally, moderate- to large-sized host sites require on-site maintenance for the network routing equipment and computers. At universities and colleges, this activity generally falls under the administration of the computing center and/ or the campus telephone services administrator. As the network decentralizes, there will be more opportunities for technical support positions within specific disciplinary areas of the university and also within commercial firms that become connected to the network.

Programming Skills

Designing new tools for use on the network is an important role for computing professionals. As the network advances, protocols mature, and new capabilities become possible, new tools will be required to interact with the network. These tools must be created by skillful computer professionals.

Even with readily available access to openly published standards such as the Internet Requests for Comments (RFCs) (see Chapter Three for more information on RFCs), most users on the network lack the skills required to code their own applications. As it grows, the network provides many challenges for the design and testing of interoperable computing systems. In a networked environment it is no longer sufficient for a program to execute properly on a single computer. If the program is to interact with other hosts on the network, it must interoperate with other applications on those hosts. This inter-operation can tremendously complicate the design and testing of new systems. Thus, programming in a networked environment offers new challenges to computing professionals.

The Educator and the Psychologist

There are roles and challenges in the cognitive sciences as well. A tremendous opportunity for educators and psychologists to play a role in the emerging network marketplace exists as younger generations of students appear. New generations of students may be required to know how to use the network to locate data and communicate in order to be competitive. Clearly, the network emphasizes the responsbility of educators in all disciplines to promote information literacy. And those who understand cognition will continue to design more effective interfaces to the network and the resources therein.

The current rate of change in network technology (and in the computing industry in general) provides an opportunity for network-literate educators to train new network users, especially in institutions of higher education, for a long period of time to come.

The Businessperson/Entreprenuer

If it is true that a new market in networked information is appearing, there will be a need for persons with fiscal, management, and marketing skills to play administrative roles for both consumers and sellers in the market. New mechanisms for achieving equity between costs of distribution and expected returns to owners of data must be designed and implemented in the network marketplace. While not all entreprenuers will be sucessful, many will find the opportunities worth the risks.

Other Issues

There are many other peripheral issues to be explored. In a work of this scope, it is not possible to fully explore all of the relevant and tangential issues. Each of these issues have generated their own books and professional symposia; we merely present the topics here for your further consideration.

- **The Future of Library Schools and the Library Profession.**
  Although this appears to be a time of great opportunity for professional librarians, it has also been a period of dramatic change that challenges library schools to remain competitive. Many schools have been closed in recent years, and there is some uncertainty as to what direction the curriculum of the remaining schools should take.

- **System Security.**
  The issues involved in building secure systems in the networked environment are many and varied. It is particularly important to have a secure system if the system is designed to be openly available on the network—which is common for online library systems. Securing the operating systems of these computers, as well as the integrity of the data being transmitted over the network, is extremely important. Without this security, there can be no confidence in the network as a source of information.

- **Transborder Data Flow.**
  An issue related to security is transborder data flow. Networks often transcend man-made boundaries such as national borders and corporate affiliations. How do we ensure that the data being used in a networked system is accessible only to authorized individuals?

- **The Internet Standards Process.**
  Currently, the process being used to develop system and network standards in the Internet is distinctly different from the process employed in other markets. While the Internet RFC process accommodates rapid development and testing of systems, it does not incorporate the wider marketplace viewpoint employed by the more formal processes of the American National Standards Institute or the National Information Standards Organization. Is there a level playing field for all potential players? Are the standards being developed sufficiently robust?

Conclusion

Our objective in writing this work was to provide you, the new network user, with both a theoretical and a practical framework for understanding the existing Internet. If we have accomplished that objective, you will have begun to recognize the enormous potential present in the emerging high-performance computing and networking marketplace. Many librarians and educators stand to benefit a great deal from continued development of high-performance computing and networking. And yet, those changes do not always come easily.

We close with a metaphor of the current networking community originally put forth by Paul Evan Peters, the director of CNI. Peters notes that the stages of network development strongly resemble the later periods of the Stone Age. It is up to us whether we follow this metaphor to a more civilized network world. There are significant barriers to fulfilling this vision of an information society, many of which have been suggested in this final chapter. However, we believe that the challenges can be overcome. Those of us currently in the network, and those to come, will be the ones to fulfill this vision.

Paleolithic to Paleoelectronic

In the Paleolithic era, humans engaged in crude behavior and predatory activities. They were hunter-gatherers—wandering the ancient terrain in search of sustenance.

We are currently witnessing the Paleoelectronic era. The true pioneers of the network—sometimes referred to as "Internauts"—are roaming the network even as you read. They engage in archaic rituals, and seek for bits and bytes of data in the distant watering holes of the network. The very nature of network data storage and organization forces these Internauts to engage in predatory activities of an electronic nature. They hunt for pieces of information, and gather them together to assemble other works. These works are then passed on as their own. There is little regard for "civilized" activity when you live in the wilderness.

Mesolithic to Mesoelectronic

In the Mesolithic era, humans began to band together into groups or tribes. They became more agrarian as they realized that some foods were easier to produce than to harvest in the wild. Crude stone tools were developed to aid in hunting and farming.

As we enter the Mesoelectronic era, networkers will form coalitions and other associations which will represent their common interests even when individually they have competing interests at stake. Crude networking tools, such as Telnet and FTP, will assist us to be more productive in this networking. Those tools will spread rapidly throughout the network community as people learn of them. In some locations, people on the network will learn to manage data in styles considered more agrarian. Rather than endlessly stalking the network in search of small pieces of data, these innovative individuals will learn to "grow" their own data locally.

Neolithic to Neoelectronic

In the Neolithic era, humans developed fine tools which were superior to the stone knives of their ancestors. Finer tools and more productive methods of farming permitted the sustenance of a greater number of humans in the villages. The birth of civilization, with a recognizable social order began to occur.

When we arrive in the Neoelectronic era, we will have developed sophisticated network agents to be sent into the network to search and retrieve data with a high level of precision and recall. High-speed bandwidths will permit greater amounts of data to be delivered and processed than ever previously conceived. Available data will no longer be limited to simple text in eighty-character terminal format; multimedia information will be available from a wide variety of sources and will be easily processed using powerful computing tools in our homes, our offices, and in our transportation systems. As the tools become more refined, more timely, and more cost effective, the virtual space will begin to support a greater number of individuals. The wide availability of information in the market will lead to a new age of enlightenment.

Notes

1. John Waiblinger, communication during the Coalition for Networked Information's 1992 Spring Task Force meeting, Sheraton City Centre, Washington, D.C., March 24-25, 1992.
2. Ibid.
3. *New York Times*, 9 June 1992. sec. D, page 1, column 1
4. Ibid, page 1, column 5
5. An interesting set of articles on this topic recently appeared in the September 1992 issue of *MacWorld* magazine, which focused on technology in education.

Bibliography

Arms, C. R., ed. 1990. *Campus Strategies for Libraries and Electronic Information.* Bedford, Mass: Digital Press.

Arms, C. R. 1990. "Using the National Networks: BITNET and the Internet." *Online* 14(5): 24-29.

Association of Research Libraries. 1991. *Linking Researchers and Resources: The Emerging Information Infrastructure and the NREN Proposal.* Washington: ARL.

Association of Research Libraries (1990. *Proposal for an ARL/CAUSE/EDUCOM Coalition for Networked Information.* Washington: ARL.

Bailey, C. W., Jr. 1991. "Electronic (online) publishing in action . . . the Public Access Computer Systems review and other electronic serials." *Online* 15: 28-35.

Bailey, C. W., Jr. 1990. "The Public-Access Computer Systems Forum: A computer conference on BITNET." *Library Software Review* 9: 71-74.

Barron, B. 1992. *UNT's Accessing On-line Bibliographic Databases.* Denton, TX: University of North Texas. (See Chapter 5)

Blau, A. 1992. "Getting a handle on the future of the NSFNet. EFFector." *Online* 3 (2). (Available via anonymous ftp from ftp.eff.org.)

Bloch, E. 1988. "A national network: today's reality, tomorrows's vision, part 1." *EDUCOM Bulletin* 23(2/3): 11-13.

Bohl, M. 1990. *Essentials of Information Processing.* New York: Macmillan.

Boucher, R. 1992. "The challenge of transition: Management of the NREN is a concept that brings complexity with no good models." *EDUCOM Review* 27(5): 30-35.

Brandt, D. S. 1992. "Information development—collection issues and campus wide systems." *Academic and Library Computing* 9(8): 23-28.

Britten, W. A. 1990. "BITNET and the Internet: scholarly networks for librarians." *College and Research Libraries News* 51(2): 103-107.

Brown, A. 1992. "Whither regional networks." *Electronic Networking: Research, Applications, and Policy* 2(3): 5-6.

Brownrigg, E. B. 1990. "Developing the information superhighway: Issues for libraries." In C. A. Parkhurst, ed., *Library Perspectives on NREN: The National Research and Education Network.* Chicago: American Library Association, Library and Information Technology Association.

Catlett, C. E. 1989. "The NSFNET: Beginnings of a national research Internet." *Academic Computing* 3: 19-21, 59-64.

Chapin, A. L. 1992. "The Internet Architecture Board and the future of the Internet." *EDUCOM Review* 27(5): 42-45.

Cisler, S. 1990. "NREN: the National Research and Education Network." *LITA Newsletter* 40, 11(2): 1-3.

Cisler, S. 1991. "NREN update: More meetings and new tools." *Database* (April): 96-98.

Cleveland, G. 1991. *Research Networks and Libraries: Applications and Issues for a Global Information Network.* Ottawa: IFLA International Office for UDT, National Library of Canada.

Cline, N. 1990. "Information resources and the National Network." *EDUCOM Review* 25(2): 30-34.

Dempsey, L. 1991. *Libraries, Networks and OSI: A Review with a Report on North American Developments.* Bath, United Kingdom: UK Office of Library Networking.

Dern, D. 1992. "Plugging into the Internet: The range of options for Internet access is almost as broad as the range of Internet resources." *BYTE* 17(10): 149-152, 156.

Deutsch, P. 1992. "Resource discovery in an Internet environment: The Archie approach." *Electronic Networking: Research, Applications, and Policy* 2(1): 45-51.

Duderstadt, J. J. 1992. "An information highway to the future." *EDUCOM Review* 27(5): 36-41.

Eldred, S. M., and McGill, M. J. 1992. "Commercialization of the Internet/NREN: Introduction." *Electronic Networking: Research, Applications, and Policy* 2(3): 2-4.

Estrada, S. 1992. "Commericialization and the Commercial Internet Exchange: How the CIX can help further the commercialization of the Internet." *Electronic Networking: Research, Applications, and Policy* 2(3): 24-28.

Farley, L., ed. 1991. *Library Resources on the Internet: Strategies for Selection and Use.* Chicago: ALA, Reference and Adult Services Division, Machine-Assisted Reference Section, Direct Patron Access to Computer-Based Reference Systems Committee. (See Chapter 5)

Fisher, S. 1991. "Whither NREN?" *BYTE* (July): 181-190.

Frey, D., and Adams, R. 1990. *!%@:: A Directory of Electronic Mail Addressing and Networks.* 2nd ed. Sebastopol, CA: O'Reilly & Assoc.

Gore, A. 1989. "The information superhighways of tomorrow." *Academic Computing* 4 (November): 30-31.

Gore, A. J. 1992. "The Information Infrastructure and Technology Act." *EDUCOM Review* 27(5): 27-29.

Hill, J. M. 1992. "The X.500 directory service: A discussion of the concerns raised by the existence of a global directory." *Electronic Networking: Research, Applications, and Policy* 2(1): 24-29.

Jacobsen, O. J. 1988. "Information on TCP/IP." *ConneXions—The Interoperability Report* 2(July): 14-15.

Kahle, B. 1991. *An Information System for Corporate Users: Wide Area Information Servers.* Cambridge, MA: Thinking Machines Corporation.

Kahle, B. 1992. "Wide area information servers: An executive information system for unstructured files." *Electronic Networking: Research, Applications, and Policy* 2 (1): 59-68.

Kalin, S. W., and Tennant, R. 1991. "Beyond OPACs . . . the wealth of information resources on the Internet." *Database* 14(4): 28-33.

Kantor, B., and Lapsley, P. 1986. Network News Transfer Protocol: A Proposed Standard for the Stream-Based Transmission of News. RFC977.

Karraker, R. 1991. "Highways of the mind, or toll roads between information castles." *Whole Earth Review: Access to Tools and Ideas* 70 (Spring): 4-11.

Kehoe, B. P. 1992. *Zen and the Art of the Internet.* Englewood Cliffs, NJ: Prentice Hall.

Kibbey, M., and Evans, N. H. 1989. "The network is the library." *EDUCOM Review* 24(3): 15-20.

Krol, E. 1992. *The Whole Internet: User's Guide and Catalog.* Sebastopol, CA: O'Reilly & Assoc.

Langschied, L. 1991. "The changing shape of the electronic journal." *Serials Review* 17(3) (Fall): 7-14.

LaQuey, T. L. 1989. "Networks for academics." *Academic Computing* 4(3) (November): 32-39.

LaQuey, T. 1990. *The User's Directory of Computer Networks.* Bedford, MA: Digital Press.

LaQuey, T., and Ryer, J. C. 1992. *The Internet Companion: A Beginner's Guide to Global Networking.* Reading, MA: Addison-Wesley.

Lottor, M. K. 1992. Internet Growth (1981-1991). RFC1296.

Lynch, C. A. 1990. "The client-server model in information retrieval." M. Dillon, ed., *Interfaces for Information Retrieval.* Westport, CT: Greenwood Press.

Lynch, C. A. 1989. "Library automation and the national research network." *EDUCOM Review* 24(3): 21-26.

Lynch, C. A. 1989. "Linking library automation systems in the Internet: Functional requirements, planning, and policy issues." *Library Hi Tech* 7(4): 7-18.

Lynch, C. A., and Preston, C. M. 1990. "Internet access to information resources." *Annual Review of Information Science and Technology (ARIST)*: 26, 263-312.

Machovec, G. S. 1990. "Internet access to library online catalogs." *Online Libraries and Microcomputers* 8(1): 1-4. (Accessible via telnet to host carl.pac.org, in the database Online Libraries)

Machovec, G. S. 1989. "TCP/IP and OSI: Networking dissimilar systems: Implications for libraries." *Online Libraries and Microcomputers* 7(6-7): 1-4. (Accessible via telnet to host carl.pac.org, in the database Online Libraries)

Machovec, G. S. 1990. *Telecommunications and Networking Glossary.* Chicago: American Library Association.

Malmud, C. 1992. *Exploring the Internet: A Technical Travelogue.* Englewood Cliffs, NJ: Prentice Hall.

Maloff, J. H. 1992. "Selling Internet service: An ancient art form on a new canvas." *Electronic Networking: Research, Applications, and Policy* 2(3).

Marine, A. 1992. *Internet: Getting Started.* Menlo Park, CA: SRI International.

McClure, C. R. 1991. *The National Research and Education Network (NREN): Research and Policy Perspectives.* New York: Ablex.

McGill, M. 1989. "Z39.50 benefits for designers and users." *EDUCOM Review* 24 (Fall): 27-30.

Morris, D. E. 1989. "Electronic information and technology: Impact and potential for academic libraries." *College and Research Libraries* 50(1): 56-64.

Neubauer, K. W. 1990. *European Library Networks.* Norwood, N.J.: Ablex.

Nielsen, B. 1990. "Finding it on the Internet: The next challenge for librarianship." *Database* 13: 105-107.

Osburn, C. B. 1989. "The structuring of the scholarly communication system." *College and Research Libraries* 50(3): 277-286.

Parkhurst, C. A. 1990. *Library Perspectives on NREN: The National Research and Education Network.* Chicago: American Library Associaton, Library and Information Technology Association.

Postel, J. 1991. IAB Official Protocol Standards. RFC1250.

Postel, J. 1982. Simple Mail Transfer Protocol. RFC821.

Postel, J., and Reynolds, J. 1985. File Transfer Protocol (FTP). RFC959.

Postel, J., and Reynolds, J. 1983. Telnet Protocol Specifications. RFC854.

Quarterman, J. S. 1989. "Etiquette and ethics." *ConneXions—The Interoperability Report* 3(4)(March): 12-16.

Quarterman, J. S. 1989. "Mail through the Matrix." *ConneXions—The Interoperability Report* 3(2): 10-15.

Quarterman, J. S. 1990. *The Matrix: Computer Networks and Conferencing Systems Worldwide.* Bedford, MA: Digital Press.

Quarterman, J. S., and Wilhelm, S. 1992. *The Open Standards Puzzle.* Reading, MA: Addison-Wesley.

Rapaport, M. 1991. *Computer Mediated Communications: Bulletin Boards, Computer Conferencing, Electronic Mail, and Information Retrieval.* New York: Wiley.

Reynolds, D. J. 1991. *Citizen Rights and Access to Electronic Information: A collection of background essays prepared for the 1991 LITA president's program.* Chicago: American Library Association, Library and Information Technology Association.

Rose, M. T. 1989. *The Open Book: A Practical Perspective on OSI.* Englewood Cliffs, NJ: Prentice Hall.

Saule, M. (1990. "Research and educational networking: A bibliography." In C. A. Parkhurst, ed., *Library Perspectives on NREN: The National Research and Education Network.* (pp.67-68.) Chicago: ALA, Library and Information Technology Association.

Shapiro, N. Z., and Anderson, R. H. 1985. *Toward an Ethics and Etiquette for Electronic Mail.* Santa Monica, CA: Rand Corporation.

Sloan, B. G. 1990. *Linked Systems for Resource Sharing.* Boston, Mass: G.K. Hall.

Sproull, L. A. K. 1991. *Connections: New Ways of Working in the Networked Organization.* Cambridge, MA: MIT Press.

St. George, A., and Larsen, R. 1991. *Internet-Accessible Library Catalogs and Databases.* Albuquerque, NM: University of New Mexico. (Published concurrently in College Park, MD. See Chapter Five for details on obtaining this publication electronically.)

Stahl, J. N. 1990. "Using the Internet to access CARL and other electronic information systems." *Science and Technology Libraries* (US) 11(1): 19-30.

Strangelove, M., and Kovacs, D. K. (1991. *Directory of Electronic Journals, Newsletters and Scholarly Discussion Lists.* Washington: Association of Research Libraries. (For information on obtaining this directory via e-mail, consult Chapter Four.)

Sugnet, C. E. 1988. "Networking in transition: Current and future issues." *Library Hi Tech* 6(3): 101-119.

Tennant, R., Ober, J., and Lipow, A. G. 1992. *Crossing the Internet Threshhold: An Instructional Handbook.* San Carlos, CA: Library Solutions Press.

Tillman, H. 1992. "Internet restrictions: Why you can't or shouldn't access or do something." *Internet World* 3(7): 11-12.

Van Houweling, D. E. 1987. "The information network: Its structure and role in higher education." *Library Hi Tech* 5(2): 7-17.

Van Houweling, D. E. 1989. "The national network: A national interest." *EDUCOM Review* 24(Summer): 14-18.

Weingarten, F. 1991. "Five steps to NREN enlightenment." *EDUCOM Review* 26 (Spring): 26-30.

Weis, A. H. 1992. "Commericialization of the Internet." *Electronic Networking: Research, Applications, and Policy* 2(3).

Williams, D. O., and Carpenter, B. E. 1992. "Data networking for the European academic and research community: Is it important?" *Electronic Networking: Research, Applications, and Policy* 2(2): 56-65.

Yavarkovsky, J. 1990. "A university-based electronic publishing network." *EDUCOM Review* 25(Fall): 14-20.

Zimmerman, D. P. 1991. The Finger User Information Protocol. RFC1288.

Index

About the Contributors

ELIZABETH LANE received her M.L.S. from the University of Michigan in 1987. She served as a Library of Congress intern from 1987-88, and then as a bibliographer in the Congressional Research Service. She left LC in 1989 to become the computer support supervisor at Congressional Information Service. Currently, she is a doctoral student at the University of Alabama's School of Library and Information Studies, where she is studying networked information resources and computer-mediated communication. During the past two years, she has presented numerous workshops on the Internet to library and information professionals. Her first book, *Microcomputer Management and Maintenance for Libraries,* was published by Meckler in 1990.

CRAIG A. SUMMERHILL is Systems Coordinator at the Coalition for Networked Information, a joint project of the Association of Research Libraries, CAUSE, and EDUCOM that promotes the creation of and access to information resources in networked environments in order to enrich scholarship and enhance intellectual productivity. In his role as Systems Coordinator, he is chiefly responsible for the development and maintenance of the computing/networking environment in the staff offices of the Coalition for Networked Information and the Association of Research Libraries. Prior to joining the Coalition in July, 1991, Mr. Summerhill was the Assistant Systems Librarian at the Washington State University Libraries and a Resident Librarian/Visiting Lecturer with the University of Illinois at Chicago. Mr. Summerhill earned a bachelors degree in music (B.M.) from the University of Nevada-Reno in 1986, and went on to study library and information science at the College of Librarianship in Aberystwyth, Wales and the University of Michigan (M.I.L.S., 1988).